A BACK SEAT
Moment

BASED ON A TRUE STORY

CONQUERING TRAUMA AND A
GUIDANCE TO RESTORATION

DELICIA MAYES

A Back Seat Moment

Print ISBN 978-0-578-29177-2

Copyright © 2022 by Delicia Mayes
Photographs © by Delicia Mayes
Cover Artwork © by Daysha Watson from Watijii Art Store

All Rights reserved. Thank you for buying an authorized edition of this book. According to Copyright laws no part of this book may be reproduced, scanned, distributed or transmitted in any form or by any means, electronic or mechanical including photocopying or for commercial purposes without the permission of the publisher.

Unless otherwise indicated, all Scripture quotations are taken from the Holy Bible, New King James Version (NKJV). Copyright 1982 by Thomas Nelson, Inc. Used by permission. All rights reserved.

Published in the United States of America
Publishing Assistance by McCurry Ministries International

AuthorDeliciaMMayes@gmail.com

My mission is to share my true life experiences to help heal, teach and restore lives with the word of the bible.

Contents

Dedication .... *iv*

Foreword .... *vii*

Chapter 1 – The Call 1

Chapter 2 – A Mother's Load 9

Chapter 3 – Day – The Sunshine Child 17

Chapter 4 – The Meat and Potatoes 25

Chapter 5 – Eye of the Hurricane 35

Chapter 6 – Now and How Now 45

Chapter 7 – Restoration Road 57

Chapter 8 – Moving On Up 67

Chapter 9 – Strive To Be Alive 77

Chapter 10 – Begin at the End 85

About the Author *89*

Endnotes *91*

Dedication

This book is dedicated to any person that has had to experience trauma or has been pierced by its dirty claws in any form. That experience may have changed your life forever but it does not get to keep its claws in you. You made it through the rough part; you survived because you are strong! You are more than what has happened to you or your family! Yes it was traumatic BUT you beat the trauma. You have become a Conqueror of Trauma!

Dedication

All four Twinsburg families and relatives that were involved in this traumatic experience – Kelly, Cidney, Laura, Max, Sam, Scott Ligon, Laura, Courtney, Scott Spencer and Daysha…we are all one family of conquerors!

To the off duty and on duty first responders, witnesses that came to help, every doctor and nurse and social workers, Dana and team at Nurenberg Paris Lawfirm and all that were involved in any way to care for all four friends. We are thankful for you and your timely response to save their lives. You all are true heroes!

To all the people who have helped us or thought of us, thank you for your kindness. Everything you have done for us is much appreciated. To every coworker, past and current, who came to help my family, thank you for your care and compassion, which you show everyday working in the hospitals. Your caring hearts helped us survive. Metro Hospital trauma teams, Dr. Hirschfeld, Dr. Lee, CCF South Pointe Radiology Department, UH Rehabilitation Harvard, UH Parma MRI Department, Bedford/Richmond Radiology Department and Dr. Debaz, thank you all.

To my parents Derick and Janice Mayes, sister Felicia, brothers Eric and Derick Jr, daughters from another mother Theandra, Nia, Bailey, Spiritual parents Gregory and Teresa McCurry, friends Laura and Don Thomas, Bonita and Mr. Cleveland, Jarrett and his mom LaTerra, Superintendent and Pastor Joseph Jackson and Grace Temple COGIC, Moma Sandra, Pastor Denise, Adreane, Barbara, Terrie, Antione and all the other church family at New Beginning Ministries, best friends Akira, Keilee, Judy, Tabitha, Latisha, Danielle, Daysha's dad Dayron and our extended families. We could not have made it through the process without your caring hearts, stepping in to help and encourage us to heal mentally, physically and spirituality. Thank you all. If I somehow missed you, please know you do matter to us too!

Foreword

It has been my pleasure to know Delicia Mayes and her Only Child Daysha since 2018 in a Relationship that has gone from mere acquaintance with her visiting the ministry to me being her Spiritual Mother and having a partnership in ministry with her. Since she and Daysha came to New Beginning Ministries, where I am the Sr. Pastor and CIO of Super Tee Inspires. I have watched her grow in her relationship with Christ Jesus to the place where her heart burns with the desire to go deeper and deeper in the knowledge of the beauty of the Lord. I have watched her family become established as godly people, and have appreciated deeply the contributions that Delica has brought to this Ministry. God has GREAT things in store for her.

I was honored that she asked me to write her foreword. In this book you will see God's hand at work, this is a true story of a tragic accident, some people lost their lives that night, but God saw fit for Daysha to be totally healed, totally restored and to tell the miraculous story about what happened that day. I remember getting the call, then seeing the mangled car on the news, thinking how did anyone survive that horrific accident. When visiting Daysha in the hospital, she was in good spirits and some of her college friends were there too. I sat with them for a few minutes, I prayed for them and on my way home I remember asking God to use this moment for his GLORY!!

One of the highlights in the book is when Delicia goes over the details of the process of a mother's heart as her daughter has several surgical procedures and is in the trauma Intensive Care Unit. This true story is heart wrenching and inspiring at the same time.

I encourage you to read this book and buy a copy for anyone that you know has Experience trauma

Teresa S. McCurry, Sr. Pastor, International Speaker, Bible Teacher & Author

Foreword

I AM HONORED TO CONTRIBUTE to this amazing testimony of strength, determination, sweat, fears and most of all faith! As Delicia's Uncle, I remember receiving the call from my sister about this accident. Immediately going online to look it up on the internet to see the vehicle wreckage then thinking; "Wow! It would literally take a miracle to just survive such a horrific accident!" When we hear about traumatic events it's certainly on another level when it hits home and it's your immediate family members involved.

In raw, detailed fashion, Delicia tells the story of what it's like to digest trauma face to face while trying to keep composed for the sake of Daysha's recovery. This emotional meal is seasoned with her faith in God's divine words written in the Holy Bible from which she draws her strength throughout.

I remember as a young child often sitting on the back porch in Cleveland (East 55th street), often looking up at the majestic stars in the sky at night in absolute awe of what beauty I was witnessing. The next morning the sun would come up and in my mind the stars simply faded away and were no longer there in the sky. It took a long time for me to realize that these stars were actually still in the sky and it was just that a bigger star (the Sun) was blinding me from seeing them. The lesson I've learned is that we are sometimes so caught up in the things that shine (Money, Cars, Houses, etc.) that most of us can't look past these materialistic things, in order to see the true natural beauty of life that's out there waiting for our eyes to behold.

Delicia's book; A Backseat Moment is a vivid reminder to us all how hard it is to digest traumatic events, and makes us realize that the monetary things we're chasing so hard for sometimes makes us forget what's truly important in this life –family!

So bucket up for A Backseat Moment, this book will take you on a raw roller coaster ride through the eye of a traumatic storm. It's a true story of intense emotions that will bring tears to your eyes, while simultaneously preparing you for some unexpected traumatic events. It will make you realize that God's help is always near, and He never gives you more than you can bear as the saying goes "If He brings you to it, He will also bring you through it!"

James A. Harris
PhD Candidate in Naturopathic Medicine
(specializing in Quantum Physics)

CHAPTER 1

The Call

─────❧☙─────

At 3.00 am, I woke up to several missed calls, followed by one voicemail from a restricted number. Somehow, reading a book on the couch usually puts me to sleep. I always call out my daughter's name to see if she has returned home from hanging out with her friends, but this time I didn't get an answer. I tried her cell phone, but it went straight to voicemail. She must have tried to call from the restricted number because her cell phone battery died. Sometimes, she would let me know that she would be staying the night over at her friend's house if it was too late to drive home. I thought I'd better check the voicemail message that was left because she still hadn't made it home.

On the voicemail, a woman says, "This is Jan at MG Trauma Hospital. Please give us a call regarding your daughter as soon as possible at 216-777-XXXX." That was the worst call I have ever received in my life! I knew instantly that something wasn't right.

I could not think, move or make a sound. I was in total shock! Thousands of thoughts rushed through my mind all at once. I couldn't even remember the number to call back. Heart pounding faster and faster, I had to listen to the recording for the third time before I could act. I kept listening to all the terrible thoughts that were getting louder in my head each time I attempted to get the phone number correct.

The first wave of nervousness was the kind you get if you were about to do something like skydiving for the first time. Or when you are in front of a room full of staring people, hoping you do not mess up a speech. Next came the feeling of being nauseous, sweating and instant shaking. My heart rate was beating so fast, it had to be well over 150 beats per minute (a normal heart rate range is 60 to 100 beats per minute). I was allowing my emotions to take over faster than I was allowing myself to think clearly.

My body became numb, my mind was almost caught up in a trance and nothing was really unfolding in a natural sense. This is how most people would react when first hearing of a traumatic event involving their loved ones. Finally, I paused long enough to key in the correct phone number. It rang three times. A woman answered and I said, "Hello, this is Delicia Mayes returning a call about my daughter Daysha."

The woman said, "Hi, my name is Jan and I'm the social worker here at MG Hospital. There's been a car accident and we have your daughter here."

The next feeling I got was total fear in the form of a gut punch. I was afraid to find out the bad news. It could be devastating or it could not be so bad. Of course I wanted to know about my daughter more than the fear. I could barely get the words out of my mouth as I asked her frantically, "IS SHE ALIVE????"

I am so thankful that the woman could hear my frantic tone and knew I needed to know the answer before I hung up the phone. She replied, "Yes…but you should get here as soon as possible before she goes into surgery."

The worst part of this kind of phone call is that usually, they will not give you any details over the phone or sometimes the condition of your loved one. Therefore, you can imagine how anyone could react in my shoes.

"Surgery!?!" I thought to myself. "She's never had surgery or even a broken bone in her life! How bad was this car accident?"

As a parent this is the part that you ask yourself, "Why did I let her go out with her friends? Am I still lying on the couch and having a nightmare? Is this really happening? Can things like this actually happen to MY family?"

As soon as I hung up, the fear that was already gripping me went up notches higher. A cloud of confusion, panic, guilt and crying all engulfed me at the same time. I could not remember how to put my pants on, where my shoes were, what to do next. And then, a deep, loud wailing cry came out from my belly, a feeling of overwhelming hopelessness. The, "Why is this happening to me?" thoughts grew louder. The reality settled in that this can happen to anyone and it IS happening to MY family right now!

You can watch the news, go on social media or hear about someone else's terrible trauma, but you never think it can actually happen to you in real life. I can honestly say I had never prepared myself for any kind of tragedy. Bad things can always happen but that was not high on my list of things to prepare for in the future. I was busier preparing for things like my daughter's college fund, retirement, buying a house, learning more about God, and getting ready for my future husband.

When I think in hindsight, I see that not many people are prepared for traumatic situations. Suddenly, God brought to my memory the bible verse in Ephesians 6:18. I understood the words "Be alert and always keep on praying." The truth is we have to stay prepared for anything, including tragedy. I know you're thinking, "How can I be ready for something I don't know is going to happen?" Being prepared by knowing what steps to take IF you are ever in a traumatic situation is the first step! The Bible tells us to watch and pray over your life, family, all situations and God honors HIS own words! You must know His words to repeat them back to Him in your prayers! When you know God's word and repeat it to Him, he will honor it because He does not lie or change His word as He says in Numbers 23:19.

So I immediately fell on my knees and started talking to God. I shouted, "GOD! Save my baby! Let her be okay! Please keep her protected by Your angels as she and I are your children. Let all the kids be okay! Lord, You said in Your word, 'No weapon formed against us shall prosper'"(Isaiah 54:17).

The next feelings I had were forgetfulness and panic. I looked around trying to figure out what to do next, "Umm, here are my pants and a shirt on the bed, I have got to get there quickly. What to do with these clothes?" I asked myself questions that I should have known the answers to but my mind had no focus. All I could think of was that I did not want my only child to die. And I did not want my child to be alone. I had to get myself together so I could be there for my child. I tried calling my parents and a few family members but they were asleep at that time of night.

I thought, "I know who to call spiritual dad and he will know what to do!" Apostle Greg answered with a deep sleepy voice, "Hello Dee, what's going on?"

I cried out, "Apostle, my ba ba baby...car accident. She is going into surgery in critical condition. I have to get there before they take her! Umm...I don't know where I just put my pants?"

Apostle Greg then said in a peaceful voice, "Dee, I want you to take a deep breath and calm down. Do you have someone there with you?"

I replied no, still crying uncontrollably.

He said, "Get your clothes on and get to the hospital. You know that God is in control, right? So all you have to do is trust in Him right now to do His miracles and be there for your daughter. Call me when you get there. And if you need, I can come and be with you."

Then he began saying a prayer for healing and miracles. Because he had the correct reaction to my panicking, I felt a sudden relief from pressure in my chest after we hung up the phone. Talking to him and praying actually helped to calm me down. I was reset back to focusing on the right thing, which was getting to the hospital.

Most people would call their immediate family or someone close during a tragic moment. In a crisis, you have to know the right person to call. Do not call the person who will shout or, cry, say, "Oh my goodness!" while panicking or those who enjoy hearing your misery with validation. You need the person that will give you the peace you need immediately, and pray with you enough to help you think straight. That person has to know how to handle your stress.

So I was able to focus on getting to the hospital as quickly as possible. I got dressed, ran out of the house, and drove straight to the hospital with the hazard lights on the whole time. And, yes, I did drive as fast and carefully as possible.

When I arrived at the emergency room, there was no parking. I drove around in a circle three times to find nowhere to park. Finally,

I just left my car by the building and ran inside. At the front desk there was a gentleman sitting.

I said, "Hello, I'm the parent of Daysha Watson, she's in critical condition."

He replied, "Have a seat; I will go check."

I believe that the gentleman at the emergency desk could read my facial expressions and knew to walk quickly so that I could hurry to my daughter. I couldn't sit and wait. My child was behind that desk in pain and waiting for me. I imagined my daughter crying in pain and calling my name.

"Sir, please hurry, she's about to go to surgery. I NEED to see her!" I said in a helpless voice. This is where I could tell you to have patience, stay calm, and be peaceful for the best results. But I just wanted to jump over that desk, Karate Kid Kick the man, and run down the hallway yelling, "Baby, mommy's here!" Yes, I stayed calm on the outside but my thoughts were churning on the inside.

After a ten minute wait time in what seemed like three hours, a nurse came out to take me in to see my daughter. She began explaining what I would see and her critical condition but all I heard was the sound you hear when your head is under water. Her voice was muffled and I stopped listening after her first few words. You hear the person in front of you talking and you try to listen to the explanation they are giving you. You even look them straight in the eyes and nod, yes you understood. But your mind has put their voice in a far, far away place! I tried to prepare myself to see my daughter in the worst state my mind could come up with and yet, I was still not prepared!

This is how I used to think when under stress. Our minds are powerful in how we react to things. They can wander off to all kinds of crazy thoughts if we let them. I wondered if I was really strong enough to handle what I was about to face. I let my own mind be in control. But there is another way to train your mind. The bible says to cast all our cares on Him, to cast all our worries, hurts, fears, and cares on God because He is big enough to handle all the things we cannot and He cares for us (1 Peter 5:7). That is the strength that you need right now!

August 2019 around 11:45 pm

CHAPTER 2

A Mother's Load

◦⋄◦

I**N MOVIES, THERE IS** always music selected for certain scenes to help you understand the emotions of the characters. Imagine the music from a horror movie that actually spooked you out. Imagine how you felt while it played in the background in that exact second that the scary thing was finally being revealed. That is what I heard in my head and felt in my heart while walking to my daughter's room, the longest walk ever.

The body reacts differently in every part of the situation you experience. You must stay aware of what your body is doing because you don't want to end up in the hospital as well from anxiety, too fast a heart rate, dizziness, etc. How can you help your loved one if you faint, hyperventilate, stay in shock or overreact in the situation? I noticed that I had sweaty palms, a sweaty forehead, fast heartbeat and a stress headache in the back of my eyes from crying so hard.

I continued walking with the nurse to my daughter's room. I took a very slow deep breath as we stopped in the doorway.

There she was lying flat on the emergency room bed, with a cervical collar on, face covered in blood, an open wound on her head and leg. But she was awake!

"DAYSHA!!!" I yelled. She tried to turn her head to look at me with the cervical collar on her neck.

"Hiiiii Mom," she said.

Can I tell you that was the sweetest, softest sound in the world to me! Instant joy, love, peace, self control, flooded me. I started crying again, this time a good cry. The feelings I received instantly were called the fruit of the Spirit in Galatians 5:22. They are the result of God's presence in us and let us experience the feeling of His goodness. These feelings come from within our hearts. God freely gives these fruits to anyone that wants to use them. So I used His peace and goodness at that time and it gave me great relief.

Brazilian jazz was playing from a cell phone next to her ear and two nurses were working hard to keep her comfortable. Only a nineteen year old kid with an old soul would listen to Brazilian jazz to keep herself calm.

I observed her body shivering from the shock while she was talking. "Mom, they told me I was in a car accident. Is everyone else okay?"

"I don't know yet baby, can you tell me what you remember before the accident?" I asked.

"I was sleeping. Then I woke up to my whole body hurting. I started screaming and Mick came over to me to tell me everything was going to be okay. There were four of us in the car, me, Mick, Candy and Cathy. Mom can you check to make sure they are all okay? Mom, please call everyone's parents too," she continued in a shaky voice.

"I will, baby. You just try to relax and I will find out for you." I said. Wiping the blood off her face, I was just amazed by her strength. Even in all her pain she was more concerned about her friends' well being than her own injuries. I asked the nurses to put a blanket over her to keep her warm as I carefully cleaned the blood off her face.

Mick was one of Daysha's best friends, so it was good to hear that he was well enough to check on her and tell her things were going to be okay. Mick and Daysha met when they were in third grade. I've watched them grow up together, graduate high school in 2018, work jobs together, start their first year of college and now hang out for summer break. All four friends had gone to the amusement park for the end of the summer celebration.

I asked the nurse, "Can you tell me where Mick is and how he's doing?"

The nurse replied, "No ma'am, we cannot give you any information."

Working in the hospitals for seventeen years and I forgot all about the law that was developed by the Department of Health and Human Services. There is a law called HIPAA: that stands for the Health Insurance Portability and Accountability Act. This law makes sure there is privacy for all patients. It protects the patients' medical records and other health information given to health plans, doctors, hospitals and other health care providers in the United States. So they were not allowed to tell me anything about any of Daysha's friends without their permission.

I learned that since my daughter was nineteen years old, I had no legal right to get any information about her medical care. I could not believe it. I am her mother and even though I pay for her health insurance, I had no legal rights to have any say whatsoever about her medical care. Can you imagine the face of a deer caught in the car headlights? Yes, that was my facial expression when I realized I knew this information but somehow forgot to apply it to my own situation.

"It's time to take her into surgery. You will have to go to the waiting room," the nurse said.

"Wait, what are they operating on?" I asked.

"It is critical that we stop the bleeding in her abdomen right now," said the nurse, as she started to wheel her down a hallway.

I kissed her cheek, "Okay, okay baby girl, you come back to me! You hear me? Come back to mommy!" I said to Daysha as they took her away.

She replied, "I will mommy."

This triggered a new set of emotions in me! It was like I'd just taken my first savory bite of my favorite snack, then BOOM someone takes the whole bag away while I'm chewing!

I went out to the waiting area where my parents were waiting for me. I somehow managed to leave voicemail messages for my parents, sister, best friends, and Daysha's dad, though I do not remember if I left messages or not. Having a support system is just as important as knowing how to handle your stress. They can help keep you calm, get you food to reserve your energy, and pray with you during the wait time. I had my parents Janice and Derick Mayes who were great supporters but, more importantly, faithful prayer warriors. They hugged me and sat down to talk. Shortly after, my sister Felicia came into the waiting room too.

Here is where your friends and family will ask you 50 million questions. Your phone will start to ring and text messages appear constantly. Try to remember they are all worried too. Don't allow yourself to get frustrated, angry or argumentative. Try to give details to one specific person that you can trust, so that they can relay the message to others for you. You may even want to hand over your cell phone to them for a little while. It is helpful to keep your mind on positive thoughts. This will definitely avoid any arguments or outbursts of emotion you are dealing with at the time. Take a deep breath in, blow it out and continue being as calm as possible; but definitely keep breathing!

Some people would ask why did God allow this bad thing to happen to me? Well, God does not want bad things to happen to any of us. In fact, He wants us all to have good experiences. Unfortunately, there are some people who choose freely on their own will to do the opposite of good, which results in consequences. This is the cause and effect lesson that we all learned in school. But know that God is working for your good in your situation. His plans are to take this terrible situation that has happened to you and bring something good out of it just because you believe that He can do it. He gives us this assurance in Jeremiah 29:11, "For I know the plans I have for you… plans to prosper you and not to harm you, plans to give you hope and a future."

God loves to prove that the words He spoke in the bible are still true today. It was a long wait in that room, but having my family there was a great help.

I had not realized that my cell phone had so many missed calls. It rang again, and I answered, "Hello?"

"Hello, Ms. Mayes, this is Detective Cortez on the case that involves your daughter. How is she doing ma'am?" said a man with a deep raspy voice.

"You're the detective? She's in surgery, sir! Can you please tell me what happened?" I asked.

"Ma'am, we're working really hard to get all the facts. So far, we know a man got onto the freeway exit at West 25th and drove the highway heading westbound on I-90 East the wrong way. We think he was driving at 100mph when he crashed head on into the car that your daughter and her friends were driving in. The driver may have been drunk. The wrong-way driver and one of your daughter's friends Candy is now deceased. We are trying to get a hold of Candy's parents. Do you have Candy's parents' phone number?" the detective asked all in one breath.

"Oh my goodness! Her friend Candy and the drunk driver are deceased! No, I don't have her parents' number right now but I will try to find it, sir," I replied, crying and in shock from the news.

"This number I called from is my personal cell phone number. Please save my number and call me back if you have any questions at all. I will keep in touch with you to update you with any information," the detective said.

"Okay, and I'll try to find Candy's parents' phone number," I said before hanging up. That phone call made me realize Daysha's injuries and surgery were even worse than I thought. My sister Felicia and I began searching for any friends on my daughter's social media that connected to the friends that were in the car crash. We left text messages to several people trying to get any information we could.

This was a hard lesson that I learned as a mother. With today's society, everything is so fast and easy at the touch of a button. I can truly say that I had slacked in memorizing phone numbers, and keeping in touch with my daughter's friends' parents. Please always have the phone numbers of your child's friends, their family or someone you can contact in case of an emergency. Also have access to your child's backup records online with the cell phone company. Of course, I had talked to her best friend Mick's parents before because Daysha had spent the night over their house plenty of times, but I did not have their phone numbers. I could not reach anyone, especially at 5.00 am.

Thank goodness my sister put on her detective brain and found Candy's old social media account that said she worked at the Breakfast restaurant! We called the Breakfast restaurant and asked for Candy's emergency contact. The people at the Breakfast restaurant stated they could not give out that information but could relay a message. I told them that it was an emergency and Candy had been in a car accident at MG Hospital. It felt so good to be able to help even if that was little to nothing. I then called detective Cortez back to tell him what I had done.

"Oh NO!!! Please tell me you didn't tell them that Candy passed away? We do not give that kind of information out over a phone call. We send an officer out to the parents' house to be there when we give them this kind of information."

"No sir, I only told them it was an emergency because of a car accident. I'm sorry I thought I was helping," I replied.

"Okay, Can you give me the Breakfast restaurant's number so I can call them right away? If there's anything else please contact me first," said the detective.

I hung up and sat there thinking about what Candy's poor parents would be going through soon. I was still in disbelief that my child's friend just passed away. But even though my mind was stressed out, I quietly prayed to God that everything would end well. All the children and families involved need prayer for strength right now.

It was so silent in the emergency waiting room. My family and I sat there waiting silently for news of Daysha's surgery.

CHAPTER **3**

Day – The Sunshine Child

Daysha age 10 at Grand Central Park NY

"It's always something, to know you've done the most you could. But, don't leave off hoping, or it's of no use doing anything. Hope, hope to the last!" —Charles Dickens.

Hope is a precious gift God gave us. When facing such a difficult time, hope takes us to the next minute, day, week, and month.

As I sat quietly in that waiting room, my thoughts began to drift to the time when I had my precious Daysha.

There's a story from the bible about a woman named Hannah who was barren. She cried out to God for a son. She prayed that if He would just bless her with a son, she would raise that child to honor and serve God for the rest of his life. I loved that story so much because God knew it was her heart's desire to have a child. He blessed her with a son named Samuel. And in return she kept her promise and gave her son back to God to serve him and work in the ministry at a young age (1 Samuel 1:1-28).

When I became pregnant, I asked God to always protect my child and bless her with His favor. And, in return, I would raise her to honor the Lord and give her life back to him. This was my agreement with God.

Daysha was born 6 pounds, 7 ounces and 19.5 inches long in October of 1999. She was so small that I could hold her in one hand. In the hospital's "baby's first picture" she had a curly afro, lips blowing a kiss and her pinky finger up. My daughter was definitely full of personality! We gave her the nickname Day because of her warm smile and ability to brighten up a whole room as she entered. When I was pregnant, I often had a weird ticklish sensation on the bottom right of the inside of my stomach. The ultrasound confirmed that it was her head. I knew that she had a full head of hair as she rubbed it against the inside of my stomach. I imagined her cracking up laughing as she knew it tickled me and I could not do a thing about it.

I often played classical music and put the radio close to my stomach so she could hear the sounds. I read somewhere about research that was done on children that listened to classical music while inside the mother's stomach. All of those children were very smart, successful, and played a musical instrument as they grew older.

I found that the library was the best place for her learning, interacting with other children and helping her develop skills from three months to school age. I kept her involved in all the library activities and the bonus for parents is that it was always FREE! From the young age of three years old, she started asking to wear her hair in an afro. She loved to draw and color everything rainbow style. It was her favorite thing to do all the time. I can say that Daysha had an artistic eye that will make you sit and wonder how she saw the things she drew. She was always creative with anything in arts, crafts, and projects. She loved all kinds of music from the 1930s to 1990s. And, even to this day, she's fascinated with Disney movies or classics that I grew up watching in the 80s and 90s.

I remember her preschool teacher saying, "Your daughter goes to every new student and gives them a welcome hug just to make them feel okay. She would tell them it would be okay and not to cry after their parents left them." She has that gift of making you feel comfortable and accepting of a person just the way they are without judging or trying to change them. That is why she has lifetime friendships to this very day. They would always say she is so nice and they like that they can just be themselves around Daysha.

I have always wanted my daughter to be better than I was in life as most parents do. I made sure she experienced all the things I wanted to but could not do growing up. We moved out to Twinsburg, Ohio, because of the excellent school system, diversity of people who lived in the city and better opportunities in life. This expanded her horizon to other cultures as well. She was put into honors classes by first grade. In fourth grade there was a world festival that her elementary class participated in for a week. Each day was a different culture to learn about. This all happened because Daysha's teacher had just come back from visiting China. The children got to see her dress up in a Hanfu, eat authentic food and learn about different countries. One day after the festival, I went downstairs and there were post it notes all over the house. They were in the kitchen, on the stove, cabinets, walls and doors. Each note had some Chinese characters on it.

I asked, "Daysha, what's all this and what does it say?"

She replied, "Mommy, I'm learning Chinese!"

My child had taken out a book from the library about Asian cultures and languages. I could not even get mad. So I smiled and said, "Okay baby girl, if that's what you want, we're going to get you all the help we can so you can speak Chinese."

About the same time, Daysha met a new friend named Mick. He was this cute little boy with the biggest smile. He had the same personality as Daysha. He and his family had just moved to Twinsburg from Texas. Daysha and Mick became close friends quickly. She would come home to tell me a story about what she and Mick did in school. They would ask if they could hang out together on weekends. She even tried to share some of his love for vegetarian lunches he brought to school. I soon realized that these two kids loved being around each other!

By junior high school I began to think that Mick had a crush on my daughter or vice versa. Daysha laughed when I asked her if they were dating. She replied, "Mom no, we're just friends! Mick is gay but please don't tell his secret." Daysha still had that loving heart to show a person that they were loved without any differences or judgments. I was so relieved! It did surprise me at how my own daughter taught me a lesson. I learned to not change my love towards a person regardless of my opinion of their situation. Treat people with the same love even after you know their secrets. So many times we have our own opinions about someone's character that we end up treating them according to how WE feel instead of just loving them for who they are, not judging, but helping them through situations with love as Jesus expresses so strongly in Matthew 7:1-5.

From that time on it was okay for Mick to spend the night or just hang out over our house. Of course, as teenagers they weren't always perfect, but they were respectful to their parents. As they grew older, their friendship grew closer. Mick and Daysha were always together helping each other. They had the same circle of friends and their bond was unbreakable.

At sixteen years old Daysha had taken two years of Chinese in high school and wanted to study abroad. I told her, as a single mother we could not afford it. So Daysha researched different affordable ways she could study abroad. She found the NSLI-Y abroad study language program, which is funded by the US Department of Education. I told her to go for it just to see if we could get her in. After the phone and in-person interviews, Daysha was picked over 4000 applicants! She was going to study Mandarin abroad in Xiamen, China, for the summer of 2016. I somehow knew that she was going to go from a mother's intuition, or a prompting from the Holy Spirit.

Of course, as a parent you worry about your children. You just want to make sure that they listen to all you have taught them, that they are not naïve, and always safe. I had to trust that only

God set this up so He would supply all her needs as He promises in Philippians 4:19. And God did just that and beyond! The entire trip was paid for except for her own spending money. She went to several famous places and lived with a host family.

Daysha came home with a new outlook on how she wanted to live her life. She respected other cultures and wanted to learn more about people from different walks of life. She said that everyone should travel to another country at least once to experience cultural differences and life from their perspective. One fun fact she told me was how authentic Chinese food is healthy, not greasy. People in China eat small portions and have no clue what a fortune cookie is! Studying abroad was a life changing experience that matured her into the young adult she is today!

Daysha and Mick went to prom with their group of friends in a limo in June 2018. As they took pictures outside my house, I remembered that little cute, blond haired boy with a heartwarming smile, and my baby girl with an afro as if they were still seven years old. Time just keeps moving before you realize how many years have passed. Shortly after prom was graduation time for Twinsburg High School Class of 2018. Daysha decided she was ready to explore college life in St. Petersburg, Florida. This would be her first time living on her own so far from family and friends. I figured since she showed me she could be responsible in China, I could trust her in Florida. Yes, it was still a challenge for me since she's my only child but we talked often…like every three days. Even with her so far away, she kept her close bond with Mick and a few other friends.

After her first year as a freshman in college, Daysha came home for the summer. I could not believe I had a nineteen year old young adult child. She spent the summer having fun with family, hanging with Mick who introduced her to Candy, Cathy and a few other friends. They exchanged stories of their first time college experiences and what they were planning to do for the next summer.

Two weeks before Daysha was to go back to college in Florida, she asked if she could go with Mick, Candy and Cathy to the amusement park for an end of the summer celebration. I told her she did not have any money to go and she had to be responsible. Mick really wanted Daysha to go, so he decided to pay her way into the park just so they could have a fun day together. Well how could I say no to such a nice young man.

On Sunday morning August 4, 2019, Daysha decided to come to morning church service with me. It's not easy to get some teens or young adults to be excited about going to church these days. The fact that Daysha wanted to come to church with me made me happy. She did not want to drive her car to the amusement park after church either, so she rode with me.

Daysha told Mick to pick her up after the church service. I was so happy to see that Daysha wanted to go to church at first, but to actually see her enjoying praise and worship made my heart melt. As Apostle Greg was closing his sermon, he asked a question that stuck in my head, "What would you do if God asked for your Isaac?" There is a famous bible story of how God told Abraham to use his son Isaac whom he dearly loved as a burnt offering to worship the Lord. Then the Lord stopped Abraham right before he was about to kill his son and provided a ram in the bush as a sacrifice instead. Abraham was counted as righteous and trustworthy in the Lord's eyes because of his obedience (Genesis 22:1-19). The Lord then blessed Abraham beyond his dreams. This question stuck in my head.

Apostle Greg explained that your Isaac could be anything that you cherish and love so much it could become your God or something you put first in your life. Your God could be a car, house, habit, money, person or place. I had to be honest, Daysha IS my Isaac. What would I do? Could I be obedient and trustworthy like Abraham? Would I still love the Lord and praise Him if He took my Isaac?

All these things were in my head as Daysha said, "Mom, Mick is here to pick me up, so I'm about to leave."

I replied, "Okay baby; did you enjoy church?"

Daysha replied, "Yes it was good. I will call you when we are on the way home."

I said, "Okay good. Love you baby, be safe and have fun!"

Daysha replied, "Love you too, bye mom!"

I thought to myself, "Next time I'm going to invite Mick and Daysha's other friends to church with us. They too would enjoy the loving, judgment free atmosphere here."

That was the last time my daughter and I spoke that day. At 10.00 pm Daysha texted me that they were leaving the amusement park and heading home. After receiving the text, I said a quick prayer for protection around my baby and her friends as they were traveling home. Prayer is the one thing that is always important to do as a parent. It sends the supernatural power of God out to do the job that the parent cannot do. As I waited for her to come home, I sat on the couch, started reading a book and shortly drifted off to sleep.

A BACK SEAT Moment

BASED ON A TRUE STORY

You are a trauma Conqueror!

CHAPTER 4

The Meat and Potatoes

※

> "¹⁰ fear not, for I am with you;
> be not dismayed, for I am your God;
> I will strengthen you, I will help you,
> I will uphold you with my righteous right hand." Isaiah 41:10

A LADY CAME INTO THE waiting room and walked where my family and I sat. "Family of Daysha?" she asked. I looked up with an anxious expression and said, "Yes, I am her mother. What is the update on my daughter, ma'am? Can I be with her now?"

She replied, "Hi I'm Jan, the social worker that called you. I'm so sorry for what you all are going through. Daysha is just getting out of surgery and will be taken into our Trauma Intensive Care Unit. I do need to get some information from you and you can see her soon."

"Oh thank God! Okay ma'am. I just want to be with my baby!"

Of course your mind is not thinking about any kind of paperwork at this time. I will tell you from my experience this is the best time to get it out of the way. If you do not have the mind frame to focus, then have the person that you appointed to take care of all questions and concerns help you. That person can give your insurance information to the hospital or social worker. It is a great idea to make copies of health insurance cards, HSA accounts for co-pays or medications needed, life insurance policies, car insurance policies, allergies, shot records, and any other paperwork that may be helpful. Give these papers to someone you can trust now! Do not dare wait and think, "Oh I have time to do that later," because that is exactly what I thought. The consequence of not being prepared left me hundreds and thousands of dollars in debt with medical bills. This was all because they did not have the information necessary to bill my insurance correctly. If I could do it over again, I would have been billed correctly and only have a payment plan set up for co-pays. No one told me that after the hospital stay I would get piles of medical bills in the mail from doctors that I did not recall coming into the room to see my daughter or even talk to us. No one warned me about more bills for medical equipment, supplies and transportation. Being prepared for this will eliminate extra stress.

I cannot tell you exactly what Jan the social worker said to me but I should have tried to pay attention. As she explained a list of things for our next steps, I could not focus or listen to her; instead I heard my own thoughts shouting in my mind. I had to force myself to stay focused, so I tuned in from time to time. This is definitely where I needed my emergency help person. Even with my experience in the hospital, I still did not know what to expect and when I would see my child again.

Listening to the healthcare workers as they explain information for the next steps in your situation will be vital to a successful recovery. I had to suppress the feeling of fear and keep trusting God's plan. I do not recall when but somehow, I called my best friend Keilee and Akira to begin to pray as I rushed to the hospital. I'm thankful that I have best friends that know how to intercede as prayer warriors without any questions asked. Hours later, Akira walked into the emergency room and sat next to me.

"I'm glad I found you! I was up in the surgery waiting area with all the other parents," she said. The police officers were in the surgery waiting area going over all the details of the motor vehicle accident. She filled us in on news that Mick and Cathy were still in surgery but no updates on all the questions that the other parents were asking the police to answer.

"Okay, I need to get some fresh air," I said. I had this heavy weight on my chest and could not breathe.

We walked outside and then I let out a loud cry. We began to pray, rebuking any evil that came to attack our family. Praying for the three children that were in surgery fighting for their lives decree and declare healing "by the stripes of Jesus" (Isaiah 53:5). It felt like a relief to let that out and just breathe some fresh air.

As we walked back into that emergency room, something changed. I was ready to fight and prepare myself for whatever was to come! Again having a support system is important!

Time flew by and it was about 7.00 in the morning. My parents, sister and best friend had left to get some rest. Daysha was finally out of surgery and I could go to see her. Jan the social worker came out to walk me to the ICU Trauma Unit. I still wondered how the other two surviving children were doing but could not get any information about them. By this time your whole body may feel weak and running on adrenaline. Try to stay hydrated because you definitely will not have an appetite at first.

I walked into the cold room to see my daughter lying flat on the hospital bed. It still did not seem real but it was very real. Her head was bandaged where there was an open cut, her arm was in a cast and so were both her legs in a cast and in traction. Traction is done with ropes, pulleys and weights. It slowly pulls on the broken bones so they are lined back up before having surgery.

A nurse was in the room taking vitals as I watched my daughter sleep. "Hello, I am the nurse that will be taking care of your daughter. Here is a booklet on the next steps as your daughter recovers. Is there anything that you need?" she asked.

"Thank you, I just want to know what all of her injuries are?" I asked.

The face she made was priceless, it was the "I'm so sorry to tell you face" but she knew she had to inform me. I took a pen and began to write down everything she said. If you cannot write, use your phone to record because it will come in handy when explaining these things to the lawyer.

Here were all her injuries: bleeding liver and spleen, pneumothorax of lung (lung deflation), laceration of head (scalp cut open), broken humerus and forearm (two places broken on arm), broken transverse processes of lumbar spine (sides of vertebrae in back), broken pelvis, broken sacrum (tailbone), laceration on buttocks to upper thigh (cut from metal pierced through seat), broken femur on both legs (both thigh bones), broken tibia (calf bone). Let's just take a breather for a second because those were a lot of details! Remember that the HIPAA law is always in effect, so you must be able to prove you are the Power of Attorney of the patient to get any information about your loved one. Now we can go back to the details.

The only thing Daysha had surgery on was her abdomen to stop the bleeding, so she could live. The nurse explained that she had to stay lying flat until they took her into surgery. At this time she could not be moved because she could possibly become paralyzed, and all her broken bones must stay lined up in the soft cast.

"Mom my back, ouch my back hurts please sit me up!" Daysha cried out loud.

"Baby I can't move you. Please just breathe, take deep breaths to stay calm," I said.

"Ohhh my back hurts!!! Mom help me, please," Daysha cried out loud.

Having an hourglass figure and big buttocks does not help when you have to lie flat. Because her waist and upper body is small and her buttocks are larger, it creates a gap right in the small of her back causing the spine to flex or bend. This is a very uncomfortable way to lie. The best way to relieve this is by putting a pillow under the legs to raise them so that the spine can become flat. I could not continue to see her like that and do nothing. So I put my arms around her, and lifted her up just a little to give her some relief. I do NOT recommend you do anything like me; I knew the proper way to help her without hurting or paralyzing her, I hoped.

"Ahhhh thank you, thank you so much," Daysha said.

As soon as I put her back down she was in excruciating pain again. So I should not have touched her in the first place because things got worse. This time she screamed so loud that five nurses ran into her room to see what was wrong.

"Can you please give her some medicine to ease her pain?" I asked.

It was hard enough seeing her in the hospital bed, now I had to see her in pain. I did not have time to cry or think about myself. I could only stay strong for my daughter. Be prepared for the next couple of weeks or months; they will be the toughest emotions that you will have to experience. However, keep in mind that you can do this, you are not alone and you will make it through. Remember, that you can do all things through Christ who strengthens you (Philippians 4:13).

Be aware! There is no full sleeping in a hospital. As soon as you start to rest for a while, there will be someone to wake you up to check on you. About two hours later a group of doctors walked into the room to introduce themselves. The lead doctor said hello and presented the case to the rest of the doctors. I felt like I was watching my favorite TV show *Grey's Anatomy*. When they come in and find the cure to a rare disease saving the person's life, next you see that person all well and walking out smiling. My reality settled as I realized this would be a long process. We were not on TV, and I did not know what was coming next. The doctor explained how they were planning to do several different surgeries to get Daysha stable enough to start healing. So there was a process even before she could start to fully heal. The plan was to get her back, pelvis, arm and both legs stable. To do this, they would have to put metal rods, plates, pins and screws in her body. At this point you just want your loved one to get to the healing part, so the only thing you can do is research what the doctors' plans are and give consent. I wanted to make sure she had a team of doctors that had a good experience with past trauma cases. I learned that the lead doctor was the top trauma doctor in our city.

I whispered a prayer in my heart, "God, I love you, and I trust you. Thank you for making sure that my daughter is in the hands of the best doctors.

With that prayer, I put my trust in the Lord to do the work needed through the team of doctors. Having faith while in a scary situation is actually your strength in action. Hebrews 11:1 says our faith is the confidence in what we hope for even before we actually see it.

Have you ever watched one of those ER shows or baby deliveries where they showed you everything you did not want to see but you kept watching it anyway? Remember squinting your eyes and holding your stomach as if it were you experiencing what you saw? Well, that was me with what happened next. I will never forget the excruciating screams that came from my daughter's mouth. No parent wants to witness their child hurting while you stand there and have to watch the doctors in action. Knowing the reasons why the doctors perform certain procedures can help you stay grounded and not lose your mind.

The Orthopedic Trauma surgery team of doctors were there to realign Daysha's broken legs. This must be done before surgery. They had to set them in place, move, twist and turn her legs so that they could get most of the broken bone realigned and set in place. Next they soft casted both legs and put the pulley weights back on to keep them in place. I honestly could not stay in that room and watch all of it, so I stepped out into the hallway praying for them to hurry up and finish! I have worked in Radiology and have seen all kinds of surgeries, broken bones, watched doctors reset bones back in place for patients and heard their screams. However, I could not watch my own daughter go through the same things. I truly understand why as a healthcare worker you cannot do procedures on your own family. It is just too personal. Emotions can take control and you have the possibility of messing up the actual procedure your loved one needs. This was the best option for me. Everyone is different, but make sure you know what you can handle. Have your support person with you especially at this time, if possible.

You will have mixed feelings during this process but, remember, you are not alone. I call it my "please, Lord, moment" because I think I called Him about forty times in a row. I wanted to cry out loud but I didn't have any more tears left in me. I wanted to sucker punch all of the doctors that were touching my daughter but I knew they were really trying to help save her legs so she could walk again.

I got angry at the drunk driver and myself for this whole situation but what can that do for me right now? I could feel my emotions starting to climb up a mountain of outrage. Then suddenly, I was reminded that she is still alive! She is a fighter, she is strong and she got all those qualities from me. Surely there is a reason she made it through all of this so far. I was not there for me; I was there for my daughter. I remembered that God said in Jeremiah 29:11 He has plans of good things for us all even those who don't know Him. I had to keep saying His word and focusing on the positive things to see them come true. This is your hope being activated to steady your emotional roller coaster ride. Take control of your thoughts and focus on any positive thing you can think of at that time.

Positivity is a crucial aspect of trauma recovery. In my case, it helped both my daughter and myself. My family and friends kept me company and that made things better. More so, my faith in God played a really important role in keeping my nerves to a tolerable level.

After about ten to fifteen minutes of the surgery planning, the group of doctors walked out and I ran back in the room. There was a quiet, peacefully resting Daysha due to an instant shot of medication. Finally, we can get some rest I thought as I slipped into the chair next to the bed to doze off.

It is vital to take time to rest during a traumatic experience. It helps to save the body from exhaustion and fatigue. These things lead to severe headaches, especially when there is no sleep. When the medication kicks in, patients can peacefully rest while giving the family time to wait beside them. Therefore, you should not take this time to discuss the situation or talk about other things. Use this time to get your own rest, and rejuvenate your body. You will be well rested and ready to engage with them once the patient wakes up.

CHAPTER 5

Eye of the Hurricane

☙❧

"Accidents happen" is a common phrase used but it should end with "to anyone it chooses to engulf." I say that because, after it hits you fast and heavy, you start to feel swallowed by the hurricane of horror.

I have learned the following important tips to remember throughout this traumatic process:

Yes, you are in this traumatic situation but there is a natural reaction that comes with it. It is okay to cry, be sad, upset and more. However, it is not okay to let these emotions overcome you.

Avoid staying angry about the situation and getting trapped in the "why-me" brigade. If you let this take over, all your energy might be focused on questioning the accident than the most important thing, recovery.

Don't avoid facing the situation by getting too busy with something else. Some people avoid talking about traumatic experiences and bottle everything inside. It is dangerous to live like that so please find someone to talk to.

Trauma forces you to endure emotions you would rather not feel. Getting those emotions out will help you endure throughout the process. I must thank you at this point because you have stayed with me through my daughter's traumatic experience as if you were her parent too. Can you see yourself in every part of this story as if it were happening to you? How you would handle things? What to prepare for next? Since this can happen to any one of us, I want to stress that I had no idea of all the legalities to come next, paperwork or preparedness I would need during this traumatic time. You do not get a chance to just unwind, you have to keep moving and make the best possible decisions quickly.

The good thing is YOU, yes the person reading right now, can get the chance to have an idea how to prepare in case of an emergency in your life! You can choose to get some paperwork prepared in case something happens to you or a loved one.

My dad came over to me and said, "I know there's so much going on right now, but I want you to talk to my lawyer."

I replied, "Dad! Thank you but I'm not thinking about any of that right now. I just want to know my baby will be fine." I was not thinking about our future, and I was trying to stay modest. But I am so glad that I did listen to my dad and talked to his lawyer. You want to get a lawyer involved as soon as possible. This is not to try to sue or get money just so you can have money to splurge. This is because there will be many things needed such as medical bills, medication, medical equipment, rehabilitation, and much more that cost beyond what you may make in a year's salary. A medical bill can be $100,000.00 or more just for one surgery. The lawyer starts to get your medical records and bills in order, so insurance can cover most of the cost. The good thing is, once your premium for health insurance is met, which it definitely will, your insurance pays the majority of the bill. All the years of paying into health insurance while you are working is very helpful. The lawyer also handles police reports, any persons that try to contact you or pretty much anything legal so that you can focus on your loved one instead. I later found out all the other families had lawyers too.

It was now the next day and I had not left the hospital, eaten, showered or slept past an hour. We heard rumors that all the families involved in the accident were on the same floor as Daysha. The mother of Cathy came over to introduce herself. We just hugged each other even though it was the first time we'd met. She told us that Cathy was stable and just out of surgery. She had similar injuries as Daysha that were on opposite sides as well as other injuries. That made sense because Daysha sat behind the front passenger side and Cathy sat behind the driver's side of the car. All the kids were in critical condition. Neither one of us could find Mick's room or heard from his parents. After our conversation, we exchanged phone numbers, then Cathy's mother went back to her room. We were told that Daysha was being taken to surgery to try to save both legs, left ankle, pelvis and tailbone. I walked next to her bed as she was being transported to the surgery department.

As we arrived at the elevator we saw one of her other best friends Nia and her mom. That was the first time we saw Daysha's big smile again. She was so happy to see Nia that all she could do was turn her head and keep smiling. Her friend cried and told her that she would be here when she got out.

When we arrived at the surgery department the nurses stopped before taking her into the room to let us say a quick prayer. I appreciated that so much and how they even bowed their heads to participate. Those little things I will always remember because it shows how they care to help those who are hurt. I kissed her face and said, "You make sure to come back to me! I love you baby and you are strong!"

She nodded okay and they wheeled her away. I was told the doctors were attempting to do several surgeries at one time, so this would be a long waiting process.

I had support from my parents, sister, brothers, friends, church family, her dad and his family as we were all in the waiting area. Your support system is so helpful because you will forget to shower, eat, drink, care about your cell phone or, at times, even breathe. I did not have to ask; people were so kind they would bring care packages or food to the hospital to make sure I ate. I sat in the waiting room letting my mind wonder about what was going on in the surgery room. To keep myself busy, I finally turned on my cell phone. There were so many missed calls, voicemails and text messages, too many to handle at that time. I decided to start with listening to voicemails only.

The first few messages were a few family members checking on us. The next call was Mick's mother. I remember thinking she had finally got in touch with me to tell me where they were and how he was doing. In a sweet low pitch voice she said, "Hi, this is Lauren. I just called to tell you Mick passed away during surgery last night." Next was the most heartbreaking cry; then she continued, "Please call me so I can know how Daysha is doing. Thank you."

All the breath in my body seemed to have left. I tried to inhale some air, instead tears rolled down my face so fast I could not hold my emotions. After hearing that message and instantly starting to cry out loud, I ran to the bathroom and continued crying. "Nooooooooooo! No, no, no, not Mick!" I screamed out loud and fell onto the bathroom floor. One of my family members ran into the bathroom after me to see what was wrong. My heart was pounding, I felt weakened and could barely catch my breath. I tried to say the words out loud, "Mi Mi Mi Mick is dead!" I mumbled.

I couldn't believe this was really happening to all four families involved. It was like hearing about the car accident for the first time all over again and not being able to get out of this loop. This accident was serious and life threatening. Our only two surviving children could have a chance of survival or passing away while in surgery, fighting for their lives. I was not ready for any more deaths. It is a constant battle with your own mind to not let those negative feelings and thoughts take control by constantly casting down every thought and imagination that works against God's word and making all our thoughts in life subject to Christ (2 Corinthians 10:5).

A lady from the surgery department came over to escort me to a private family room. I did not realize my crying was so loud that other families in the waiting room began to stare at us. I had just talked to him a few weeks before the accident. He came to my job to pick Daysha up so they could hang out. I stood next to him and looked up at all 6 ' 2" of him, then gave him a big hug. "Mick, you are growing some peach fuzz on your chin! I have not seen you in so long. What have you been up to?"

He laughed and said, "Ha! Yeah, I'm going for a new look. I have been doing good. I got a new car now and I'm going to Kent State College."

I said, "I'm so proud that you and Daysha are both doing good. Don't be a stranger when Daysha leaves for school and you two behave today."

He laughed and said, "Okay I will, Ms. Mayes."

My immediate family gathered in the private room as I tried to calm down to call Mick's mother back. My heart was broken for Mick's parents, Candy's parents, Cathy and her parents and my daughter, so I just kept crying. God said He will comfort the broken-hearted (Psalm 34:18). And that's what He did through my family who were all around to comfort me. As a parent it's in our DNA to be our kids' protector. So when you cannot do that parent superpower, it is hard to cope with that reality. I wanted to bust through the surgery doors just to hug and hold my baby girl and tell her, "Mommy's got you, everything will be alright!"

So the phone call to Mick's parents was tough. I called and Mick's mother answered the phone, "Hi Dee…Mick passed away during surgery last night, I just don't understand why…why did this happen? Why did that guy have to get on the freeway and drive drunk? We just wanted to check on Daysha and Cathy. How is Daysha doing?" she said.

"Aww, Lauren, you are so sweet worrying about the girls at this time. First, I am deeply sorry to hear about Mick. This is a horrific thing that we are all experiencing right now. I just can't stop crying for you guys and Candy's parents. Thank you for asking. Daysha is in her second surgery right now. They are trying to save her legs. Lauren, I am just so sorry!"

We both stayed on the phone just crying, no words were needed at that time. Lauren asked me to keep her up to date with Daysha's progress as she told me about the other families involved in this traumatic accident. She said it was on the news, so lots of people were starting to find out about the accident. The news was fast to report as the police did their investigation.

About five hours had gone by and Daysha was still in surgery. There were a few times they called us to the desk to give us an update that things were going well. During all the chaos I forgot that I had an appointment to meet with our new attorney. Remember, you cannot do everything by yourself. You may have so much going on, it's always good to have that designated person to help remind you of things, run errands, make sure your needs are met, etc. I know they sound like an assistant, right? But really if you have good family or friends they will have it in their hearts to help you through this trauma.

The attorney Diane was directed to the private family room to speak with me. She was very nice, told me about herself and made sure that she asked about Daysha before we got to any business. That made me feel much more comfortable knowing she cared, or at least was respectful. My parents were definitely there to help because my mind was all over the place. My nose was completely stopped up and my eyes were so swollen from crying I could barely keep them open to read the papers. I asked her to go over each part with me. She pulled out her paperwork and explained how everything worked.

Some helpful tips are to make sure you understand all the verbiage being said, ask questions even if the question does not sound right to you… ask! Read, read, read over everything before signing anything. Some attorneys will not have you pay anything upfront while they get your case together. Each case is different for each person's situation. After talking with the lawyer, I understood that she was taking over the stress of paperwork, and going straight to working on getting every detail of the accident, and that was okay with me.

By this time six to seven hours had passed. We finally got word that Daysha's surgery went well and they were finishing. Since she was now stabilized, they took her out of the ICU and moved her to the critical trauma floor. Everyone there to support us celebrated with hugs and smiles as they began to leave. My parents and sister headed to Daysha's new room which was in a different building. As we got there, we had to wait in the waiting room until she was able to have visitation. Usually the nurses are cleaning the person up from surgery because it can get messy. They want to make sure your loved one is presentable, all vital signs are good and the person is able to have visitors. You may wait thirty minutes to an hour before getting to see your loved one.

When we arrived at the trauma floor waiting room, there was more family and friends there to meet us. I had no idea how they knew we were there in that particular hospital or how they even found where we were in the hospital. I can say those who actually care about you or your loved ones will find a way to see you. A few more friends and family greeted me with hugs of love. I explained to them that Daysha was being taken care of as we waited.

I had gotten Candy's mother's phone number from Mick's parents. I felt in my heart that I had to call her even though we had never met before. I went to a quiet space and dialed her number. A soft voice answered, "Hello?"

I said, "Hello this is Daysha's mom, Dee. I just want you to know that I am praying for you and your family. I am so sorry about Candy."

She cried out loud and I cried along with her. I could hear the pain in her voice as she said, "I just can't believe this is real…umm, how is your daughter?"

I told her that she was just getting out of surgery. I thanked her for being concerned and told her I would keep in touch. That was the third hardest thing I experienced that day. Even though I wanted to be left alone, I was still happy my family was around. I needed them as they showed how much they cared.

Finally, after an hour's wait, we were able to go back to see my baby, only two at a time. As she was sleeping, I could only kiss her forehead to let her know mommy was right here. She had casts on each leg and one arm, and her head was bandaged. I remember in the movies seeing a person in full body cast after an accident. But this was real life and it looked exactly the same. Seeing Daysha that way started something inside of me. I was ready to fight back, to not feel depressed, defeated or helpless but determined to get her back to herself one hundred percent. My mind switched to where we were heading…down restoration road!

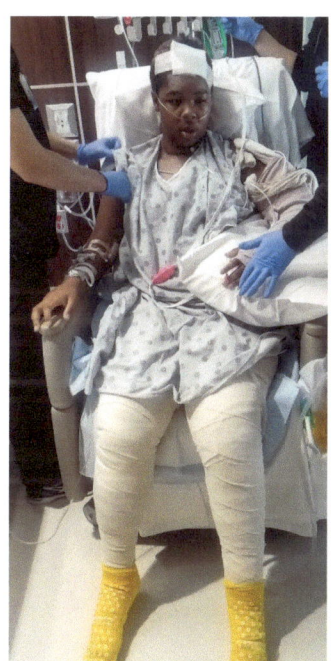 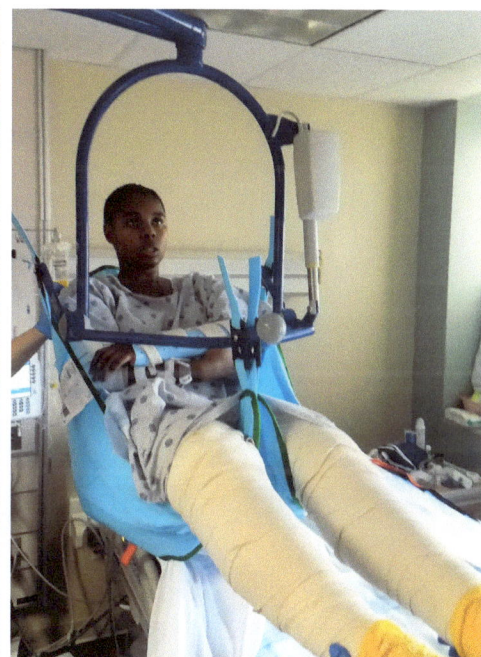

On left Daysha post surgery in ICU.
On right Daysha in Hoyer lift.

CHAPTER 6

Now and How Now

❧❦❧

Take a deep breath until you cannot breathe in any more air. Hold it for a split second, hold it, hold it, now blow all the air out. I do this sometimes to get myself relaxed or to just take a pause out of a situation. That second breath I took in felt like the fresh new air of relief.

Prayer gives assurances that God hears your request and has already been working on it because He loves you. Before you ask, God already knows the answer for your situation. The reason you must still ask Him is because it shows your confidence in Him to do what you asked for through your faith. So all you need is to have faith in Him. Hebrews 11:1 Prayer is powerful. I believe the prayers for all families involved were being heard in heaven.

Daysha's physical therapy, therapeutic art, and rehabilitation were already planned to begin a few days after her first six surgeries. I got more information about Cathy from her parents after visiting her room. We learned that Cathy had similar injuries and a number of surgeries too. Due to the force of the impact, Cathy's abdomen was cut almost in half from the seat belt, and her cervical spine was displaced. She was recovering just down the hall on the same trauma floor.

Cathy's parents and I decided together that we would not tell our daughters about Mick's or Candy's deaths until all of their surgeries were done. We wanted both girls to be in a recovery stage before they knew about their best friends. Daysha often asked how well her friends were recovering and where Mick and Candy were. I made sure all the staff, friends and family knew to not say anything about her friends yet. The only answer I could give her without lying was, "Baby girl, they are in this hospital too, but I don't have any more information that I can give you. Right now, my focus is on your healing." I could not let the words come out of my mouth that her friends had passed away and they were in the morgue of the hospital and that their poor parents were broken-hearted. I could not imagine what they were going through at this time.

I felt sad that I did not have time to sit with or show my deepest condolences to either of the parents. At the same time, I felt so grateful that my daughter and her friend had survived. I could say I was being over protective of my daughter's heart and I was being selfish too. This is because I could not bear to see her hurt anymore than she already was physically and mentally. I could not bear to see her crying from heartbreak or becoming depressed if she heard the bad news before going into surgery.

Here's the worst thought possible as a parent that ran through my mind. My heart could not take it, if I told my child the news of her best friends' deaths and she thought why was she the one that survived then get depressed or give up on life. Now that's the most honest answer that I could give as a parent. This is that secret place that I needed God to meet me in because He says in HIS strength I can do all things through Christ Jesus (Philippians 4:13). And right now I needed His mental and emotional strength.

Due to trauma, your body goes into a defense mechanism that creates a chemical stress response. This is called the fight or flight response. Our body's defense system is on high alert so we experience intense physical emotions such as fast heart rate, higher blood pressure, sweating, loss of appetite etc. Trauma affects the person involved as well as their loved ones. I did not have an appetite, sleep, shower or awareness of my exhaustion.

Daysha was not taking her pain medication as if she didn't feel any pain and mostly smiling given the current circumstances. She even asked me to cut off all her hair. During surgery they cut off her hair only where her scalp was cut so that they could stitch it back together, so we cut all her hair off with scissors. She looked like a young George Jefferson with pink hair!!! But we weren't our normal selves. The hospital has trained staff and social workers that know these signs so they would come to talk to us often. They provided us with programs for aftercare, support group information, free meal tickets, parking validation and much more. I didn't realize then how useful it was.

Every two hours there was a nurse doing rounds, different doctors checking in, labs to do blood work or even the cleaning personnel. They are working around the clock to give you the best patient care they can but remember you will not get any sleep! I made sure to watch how they worked to move Daysha safely. Only her right arm was unharmed so that she could try to help them. The nurses had to help her use the bathroom, bathe, slide onto or off the bed into the chair, take pain medication and be fed. The routine looked easy as I watched the nurses and aids use their super power. Just remember I said that, because later I will tell you it wasn't as easy as I thought when we got home! To turn her, it took two people and they had to do it very carefully. I had some knowledge of this from working in the hospital with patients but it's different when it's your own loved one. I paid close attention to what worked best with the least amount of pain to move her.

I can say this experience has made me more empathetic as a healthcare worker and appreciative of those who care for the well being of patients. I already enjoy helping people feel better but this gave me a new perspective! I understood how to give better patient care to others when they are in pain as well as after care to my daughter.

I have to tell you how God's plans are already set up to help you because He knows your ending to the situation before you even knew you had a situation. As it says in Isaiah 46:9-10, only His counsel shall stand!

Back in the fall of 2019, my Senior Pastor Teresa was preaching a sermon on the power of your faith in God. As she taught on this subject, she spoke about a new movie she had watched. The movie was based on a true story about a boy who had fallen into icy water and died for over forty-five minutes. The mother of that boy did not take death as her son's final destination. She stood over his body, prayed and spoke God's word back to him. She asked the Holy Spirit of God to bring her son back alive. Right at that moment the boy had a pulse again! After that the doctors, friends and family all said he was brain dead or would not stay alive. The mother stopped anyone who came into that hospital room from saying any negative things about her son. They looked at her like she was crazy and people felt bad for her, thinking she was delirious. But because of her faith, he is alive and well to this day!

That story stayed in my head and amazed me so much I had to go see the movie! I now understand why God allowed that movie to touch my heart. Little did I know that the summer after the movie was released, I would do just as that mother in the movie did. I did NOT allow any hospital employees, family members or friends to come into Daysha's hospital room with negative words, emotions or anything! Yes, some people said I needed to be realistic, that she would not walk normally again, she would always have pain or some kind of problems from the accident. But I did not accept any of those comments. I kept my faith! I always spoke good things around her, told her she would be back to normal or better, and encouraged her to keep on pushing, keep on trying, keep on healing and keep on thinking positive.

This is the most important thing to do when the healing process begins because it will take time to heal. Some key factors to remember are to have a positive support system. For the trauma survivor, do not isolate yourself, and be patient with yourself. Your body has changed, so take it one day at a time. Other activities that will help you to heal are meditation, music, art, support groups or start easy exercises if possible. Keep focused on positive energy around you. Yes, there will be some days you feel bad but it does not mean you have to stay in that dark place. Remember one day at a time to get back to yourself or your new self!

One day a man and woman walked into Daysha's room both smiling and saying hello. They introduced themselves as former trauma survivors. Both of them told short versions of their stories and gave encouraging words to us. Later that same week a young man walked into the room on two metal legs. He was handsome and full of personality! He smiled and introduced himself as Keith, a member of the trauma survivor team. He shared not only his traumatic story but also of his failure to follow the healing process, which made it take longer. He gave Daysha some great advice to help with lying in a hospital bed for so long. An example was that your back gets so hot and sweaty from being in bed so long. The secret is to use baby powder on it to help keep it cooled down! We found out that he had graduated from the same high school as Daysha!

This was one of the most amazing programs that the MG Trauma Hospital had to help patients cope with the situation at the time. I was very impressed with all the programs they offered. You will want to get in touch with the social workers department to get information needed for your particular situation. They will have all kinds of helpful information from places to go for after care to getting financial assistance.

Only two days after surgery, we had all kinds of visitors. I didn't know how they knew what room to come visit but I appreciated those friends and family wanting to help. Some people we had not seen in a long time came because they saw the accident on the news. That is why you may want to have a POA or family to set up privacy for your room. You can legally tell them no visitors, and give a list of family or friends that may visit you. Each person's situation varies as some people may like to have many people around. Make sure to give all copies of any legal documents from your healthcare insurance.

My immediate family noticed that I had been at the hospital since the night of the accident. I had on the same shirt, pants and flip flops for several days. I'm pretty sure I did not smell so well either! I did wipe my face off every morning but I was overdue for a shower! My sister came to stay with Daysha and told me to go home, shower and get some rest. I agreed to go home because I did need to pack so I could move into the hospital with my baby girl. It was hard to leave that room. I knew she was in good hands but I wasn't ready to leave her.

As I walked to the elevator I realized that my car had been in the emergency room parking lot way off in another building. I got home and went into the house just to stand in the shower crying. I finally had time to release some things for myself. As the person who is supporting your loved one, you need to decompress as well. No, you did not go through the trauma like your loved one, but you are experiencing the effects of the trauma too!

Stay aware of your own mental, physical and emotional health. Yes, you have to be strong for them, yes, you have to help them but you cannot help them if you are burnt out. You can even try rotating turns with other family members to help your loved one. Make sure to do a wellness check up for yourself every few days as well. You and your loved one's well being is the most important part of the process!

The physical therapy team came in to introduce themselves. There were three women that came to get Daysha up and into a wheelchair. What we did not know was that Daysha's session was happening right at that time! This would be the first time she was up since the car accident. This was both exciting and scary because we didn't know what to expect. The team explained that since she couldn't get up, or use her legs or broken arm, she would slide on a wooden board over into the wheelchair, then they would help shift her body to be comfortable. Remember, she also had staples for the cut that came from the metal bars under the seat of the car and pierced under her thigh to the buttocks. She also had some broken lumbar spine transverse processes and a head injury. When the therapy team used the transfer pads to help her sit up, she got dizzy for a second, so they had to wait.

Once she was okay, the transfer began but it was not pretty. Daysha did not know how to help move herself because she had no strength. I think that was mentally disheartening for her, and she began to cry. That was hard for me to watch since I usually help patients for a living but was not allowed to intervene with my own daughter's physical therapy session. I knew they would take good care of her. It has been proven that the faster you get out of the hospital bed after surgery, the faster your body will start to heal.

The therapy team was very nice. They helped get her all the way into the wheelchair and made her comfortable. By this time Daysha was tired but glad she could get out of her room. I was so excited that she was out of bed. I started to record her first time in the wheelchair. The therapy team said for her to stay up in the wheelchair for one hour. Then they would put her back into bed. They suggested taking her to the family waiting room where there is a big window to look outside. As we started down the hallway, Daysha asked that we slow down the wheelchair. She said that she was getting hot so we gave her a paper fan and some water. As we got to the waiting room we came to a huge window that showed the town. Daysha looked out the window for two minutes and started panicking. She cried out, "Mom take me back! Take me back to my room pleeeease! I feel dizzy and everything is going dark!" as she started crying and fanning herself. I rushed her back to the room and called the nurse.

"It's going to be okay baby! Don't cry," I said.

We rushed right back to the room and immediately called the nurse.

The nurse came into the room to help calm her down. I didn't understand why that happened without anyone preparing us for it. How long would she be like this? That was not how my daughter normally reacted. I asked God what was happening? Thinking about it now, I was just emotionally overwhelmed but had no time to cope. I did not like my daughter being that way and something needed to be done. The nurse explained that it was a normal reaction after a traumatic accident that some people experience. So there's no way of knowing if it will happen to the injured person.

The therapy team came back with a device called a Hoyer lift. They slid it underneath Daysha and lifted her in the air over to her bed, then placed her back quickly and easily. She said that was the best part of therapy; she enjoyed getting in the lift because it was like a slow roller coaster ride. Once she was in the bed, she felt good again. The physical therapy team told us they would come every day now. The first day's adventure was over.

Next came a doctor from the surgery team to check on Daysha's recovery. They checked the leg brace and all the cast. They told us the plan for her next three surgeries to save her arm and knee, then to get her into a rehabilitation center. This was good news because it meant a faster chance of recovery. Her surgery was two days later. To keep Daysha's mind on healing, an art therapist was also sent in to help. She heard that Daysha's favorite thing to do was art so this would be fun. Daysha was excited to paint and talk to the therapist as she painted an expressive picture. Daysha said, "Mom, isn't it funny that God left my right arm unharmed so that I can paint?"

I replied, "Yes, you're right! God knows you love to paint so you needed that arm." The therapist and I had talked earlier that day. She suggested telling Daysha about her friends' deaths while she was painting because it would be a way she could express her feelings. Of course my heart was broken and I was not ready to bring up this painful news. Daysha had already been asking a number of people to please tell her how all her friends were doing, but no one gave an answer.

As the therapist was talking, Daysha was painting bright flowers. My mom and sister were there for support as I said to her, "Babygirl, I want to talk to you about something important. I love you and would never lie to you but I needed to wait until your surgeries were done before I could give you this information. When the car accident happened, Candy passed away immediately. Mick was unconscious and rushed to surgery, but he passed away too. Cathy and you are the only survivors. I am so so so deeply sorry that you are just now finding out."

Daysha stayed silent as heavy tears rolled down her face. She kept painting while crying as she asked for the blue colored paint. My mother rubbed her back and said, "Daysha, I believe that when you said the first thing you remember after the car crash was Mick coming to tell you that everything would be okay, that was God allowing Mick's spirit to talk to you and let you know everything will be okay before he left this earth."

Daysha cried and said, "I knew something was wrong. I knew when nobody would answer any of my questions about them that something bad happened… but not that they were gone!"

The art therapist stepped in to say some kind words but also continued therapy with her as she painted.

Daysha made a painting of Mick's face with a teardrop on it in blue paint. The painting was so evocative. I honestly believe with all my whole heart that God allowed Mick's spirit to come to Daysha in the midst of the car crash to let her know everything WOULD be okay. It was the first thing she told me when I got to see her in the emergency room and I will never forget it! We still have that picture of Mick today.

Candy's funeral was on the same day as Daysha's arm surgery. One of my closest friends went to represent our family to support her family. I was told Candy had a glow in the dark ceremony instead of candle light, and the funeral was beautifully done. Rest in peace Candy, you lovely young lady with a smile that could light up a room. Rest in peace Mick, you handsome young man with the heart that brought so many together.

CHAPTER 7

Restoration Road

God will allow you to go through situations but restore you to greater than you were before. We knew God's restoration process had begun. As physical therapy became more intense Daysha's strength increased.

> "Will you be made whole?" John 5:6

Do you remember that song in kindergarten that we used to sing but didn't know it really would be used in life? The hip bone's connected to the thigh bone, the thigh bone's connected to the knee bone, the knee bone's connected to the leg bone, the leg bone's connected to the foot bones, now shake those bones all together! Did you just sing the song in your head like I did? I am definitely laughing right now.

Fun fact; I learned that the song is based on the bible story in Ezekiel 37:1-14 when the prophet Ezekiel visited the Valley of Dry Bones. There God told him to speak to those dry bones so they could live. The bones began to connect to one another after he prophesied to them and they got up and began to form human bodies! When one part of you is broken, the other parts step in to help without you even thinking about it. We are made in such a special way that each part of you is automatically connected to another part. I say that to remind you that healing not only takes place physically but mentally, emotionally and spirituality. We quickly learned how the broken bones in Daysha's body affected the connected bones that would take on more of the workload when trying to move her around. Her right arm gained more of that responsibility so she had to strengthen it to pull herself over. Physical therapy helps you to learn the proper way to do the movements while improving your health.

For the next few weeks, we had a good moving system and help from the nurses. Daysha began to gain strength, enough to put a little weight onto her left leg with the brace on! We took small wheelchair trips in the hallway to build her up to going back to that window. We had success from perseverance, positive encouragement and a loving team. It was time for her next surgery on her left knee. My family and I waited in the same surgery area as the last time. I recall thinking, "I pray this is the last surgery she has to get, dear Lord." My poor child went from never having a broken bone or surgery to having several. Just as I was talking to God in my head about no more surgeries for Daysha, they called me to come to the back. The surgeon had requested to talk to me before he started the surgery on Daysha.

I went back to say hello and he said, "Hello Miss, I have your daughter on the surgery table. I looked at her knee, and bent it in different ways to break up the scar tissue but it is healing fast on its own. I don't see the need to do another surgery on her. I believe she will heal fine with some hard work and exercise."

"Oh thank you God for hearing my prayer!" I gasped. "This is such good news, doctor; thank you!" He smiled and went back to cancel her surgery. The doctors and I were all amazed at her fast healing. Right there was a miracle in today's world that God did just that quickly!

When we got back to the room there was a nurse that was so sweet she brought us homemade Puerto Rican food. We felt like it was Christmas to have such yummy food for a day. People who visited would bring food in also to save our pallets from basic hospital food, as well as gifts, flowers and cards.

Daysha woke up the next day talking about a dream she had about the Pastors from our church. That same day our Senior Pastor

Teresa came to visit. She brought us some delicious food too! We were so happy just to have a home cooked meal. It was like getting a tender T-bone steak dinner! As Daysha talked with her and told her about the dream, Pastor Teresa asked her how she was feeling about things that happened. Daysha's reply was, "This is just a moment in my life. It will not always be this way."

That answer was so deep and extraordinary. To see the trauma survivor and all that she had been through and have to still go through, her attitude was so positive. Pastor Teresa was so impressed that she told us it changed her perspective on how to look at situations going forward. She even shared with Apostle Gregory about what Daysha had said and he preached about it in his next sermon! I was a proud mom that day!

Just when you get used to everything, please be aware there will be a sudden change in routine. The social worker's department came in to talk to us about moving Daysha out of the trauma hospital into rehabilitation. You must know your health insurance and what type of facilities will be accepted for payment. I was not aware of this and was told she had to go to a nursing home. I refused to move her to a nursing home and said we would wait until I saw a few of the places first. Do not let them rush you! They wanted to send Daysha out by that same week. I did not choose a place until I did my research. This gave us another week to prepare.

I talked to God about wanting her to go to the brand new Rehabilitation Center, then prayed about it even though they had already told me no. You want to pick a place that is best for you and your loved one. I had to get myself together, research and visit a few places. This process will take some time. I did this all on my own but I highly suggest you get help from your support person. I was thankful for her sister Theandra and aunt Felicia as they took turns being with Daysha while I went out to look at all the different places. I was overwhelmed with all the stress of doing this by myself. I remember going to the library just to use the computers to search for more information. As I was in the library I started to break down and cry out of the pressure of so little time. There were a few nice ladies that came over to me and just hugged me. One lady prayed for me, which gave me comfort.

Finding a nursing home was not what I wanted for my daughter. I was told if she could not bear weight on at least one leg, then she would have to go to a nursing home. The rehabilitation center is where she would get physical therapy training and occupational therapy. This was the best choice for her but my insurance only paid for certain places. It is important to keep in touch with your health insurance company because they can help give you a list of places that are within your network. This means they will cover the payments depending on what your insurance company requires, though you may have a small portion to cover as well.

Again God stepped in to ease my stress, for did He not say in His word *"Come to Me, all you who labor and are heavy laden, and I will give you rest"* (Matthew 11:28-30)? While I was out looking at different nursing homes, the surgeon had come to tell Daysha she could bear the weight on her left leg with a brace on at all times. I was so relieved and already knew the rehabilitation center that would be best for her healing process. I talked with Cathy's parents and they were experiencing the same things looking for a nice nursing home with so little time. We tried to help each other out and get the two girls in the same place. However, our insurance was totally different so we had to go to different facilities. Cathy was also set to leave the trauma hospital that same week. We finally set up transportation and Daysha left the trauma hospital after three weeks and nine surgeries!

The Rehabilitation hospital was brand new with huge private rooms and showers. We moved Daysha in and got all settled. That night was straight to work as we had to learn a new way to help her use the bathroom. She had to actually get up each time. Normally the rehab used a belt strap that goes around your back to help lift you while moving, but Daysha's back was broken so we could not use the belt. It took three nurses to help pivot her on and off the bedside commode.

On the first night Daysha and I rested well after all that hard work. We were in for a nice surprise! The next morning we woke up to a nurse smiling at us. It was 7.00 am and time to start her new daily routine. Occupational therapy taught us how to get Daysha onto the bedside toilet with as much help that she could give, brush her teeth, bathe using a bedside tube because she could not get in the shower yet. This was not easy but each day we tried a new way until we got something that worked well. Next was lunch, then Physical Therapy which was the challenge. Daysha had to try many things to gain strength to do simple things like lift her arm or turn her leg a certain way. They ended up getting her an electric wheelchair so she could get herself around the place to make her appointment times.

They make you become independent as much as you can. Sometimes you will get frustrated or disappointed but keep that push. It is the mental and physical strength needed to make it through! Your only option is to keep trying because you want to heal the proper way. You want to be able to move or do things like feed yourself again. Lastly was dinner and then her favorite part, artwork! This became her daily routine for the next few weeks. The nurses at the rehabilitation center were just as nice as those in the trauma hospital. The difference is that they have to push you to move to accelerate the healing process.

Oh boy! Did we put in hard work when moving her every time she had to go to the bathroom, a therapy session in the gym or the cafeteria to eat! This consistent movement helped her to learn how to get her body to do everyday things again. Remember to stay determined! It will not be easy but you can do this. You want your loved one to get well and heal properly one day at a time. Some tips I can give: bring your own blanket, have your own toiletries, keep yourself hydrated and eat to have energy. Take notes of everything the doctors are telling you. Ask them questions when you do not understand; it is your right to know. Stay in touch with your lawyer for updated information. Refer all calls from insurance companies to your lawyer. You can let them take care of those things, so you can focus on other things. Make sure you or your designated person get FMLA (Family and Medical Leave Act) forms from your job. You must get those in as soon as possible. You do still have to take care of all this paperwork during this traumatic experience.

The workers were happy to have a nineteen year old around for a change. She brought the fun side out of the workers with her colorful spirit and they loved all her artwork. Her painting was her personal therapy. You could see that she expressed her emotions through the pictures that she painted; they were so alive. So I began to hang them up all over her room. I literally moved into the Rehab center with my daughter. I had a small suitcase loaded with a change of clothes. The rehabilitation center usually does not have visitors stay overnight, so there is no comfortable place for you to sleep. I slept in a recliner chair next to Daysha's bed every night with as many blankets as possible. It definitely stays cold in any healthcare facility you visit. I believe all healthcare facilities have a secret thermostat company that is manufactured to have temperatures from Antarctica!!!

Daysha would wake up in the middle of the night to use the bathroom, need to turn or needed pain medication so I had to sleep light. I am thankful they understood that my daughter was not capable enough for me to leave her side. I would help her until a nurse was able to come to help us out.

Just as I was trying to figure out how to get some things done, God stepped in through so many people. God is always thinking about you even when you're not thinking about yourself. All the blessings were how we survived. (Philippians 4:19-20).

We learned that Cathy had gone to a private nursing home instead of a rehabilitation center. This was because she was still healing as well but could not bear any weight yet. All four families kept in touch with each other since the night of the accident. Candy's mother was having a difficult time after the funeral, which we understood. We kept her uplifted in prayer and called to check on her at times but wanted to, respectfully, let her have privacy to grieve and heal with time. Cathy's parents were in the same situation as we were by being at the nursing home while she was healing.

Mick's parents are strong hearted people because they put their pain to the side just to come visit Daysha with balloons and gifts. We hugged each other and cried. It was good to be around them but I know it was also hard for them to see Daysha that way, while missing their son Mick. We talked for a little while and they told us that they had just left from visiting Cathy too. They showed so much strength that it encouraged me to be just as strong and keep pushing for Daysha to heal. I have to say my feelings were all over the place. I was so happy that my daughter was still alive and that one of her friends survived because they needed each other to get through this trauma. At the same time, I felt terrible that two of her best friends had passed away and their parents were brokenhearted, which broke my heart too. I made sure to be respectful and careful of the things I said because all of our emotions were running high. As I talked to Cathy's mother she confessed feeling the same. I think it is good to be able to talk about your feelings during those hard times. Even though the parents were not in the accident, we were affected by it too.

Trauma does not care who you are, neither your age or ethnicity matter. It just wants to wreak havoc. Do not give it total power to stay in your life. When faced with trauma, I told myself to just let it go. I know, easier said than done, but that was a start for myself to be an example to my daughter so that we could move forward together.

CHAPTER 8

Moving On Up

◦₍෧·෨₎◦

D o you remember the Twilight Zone TV series? The characters would walk around wondering what strange place they were in or their surroundings were not familiar? I could hear that soundtrack playing with the man in the background saying there is a fifth dimension that we call the Twilight Zone. As I walked into our townhouse it felt so weird. It had been so long since I was in my own home. The first thing I did was fall right into my bed and enjoy the comfort of the soft cushion while my back could finally stretch out. After a month of sleeping in hospital chairs, you know that felt great!

As I lay there, that same thought would still run across my mind from time to time. Is this really happening? Is this reality? I would sometimes have to take a moment to mentally tell myself you are in the middle of this traumatic situation but things will get better. Sometimes you have to encourage yourself in order to keep pressing forward. I remember reading a bible story about King David when he was faced with a terrible calamity. His camp got burned and the women and children were taken away captive by the enemy. His men threatened to stone him but he decided to seek the Lord. He was severely distressed but he found strength in the Lord his God (1 Samuel 30:6).

I came home to rearrange the furniture. The living room would now be Daysha's new bedroom because she was about to come home next week! A hospital bed and wheelchair were being delivered today. Unfortunately my insurance did not cover a bedside toilet or the gel padded mattress. I had to pay out of pocket for a toilet online that was exactly like the one at the rehab center. I bought a cheap version of a padded mattress topper to start. Find out all details of your part of insurance that is and is not covered. Find out what payments they will make and what limitations you are given. In the long run, this will cut out any confusion or extra stress when trying to get things set up as quickly as possible. Our house was transformed in just a few hours. Everything was delivered and set up that same day. We had plenty of supplies and some space to be able to transfer her back and forth onto the hospital bed.

Daysha gained some strength from occupational and physical therapy sessions each day. The cut under her buttocks was healing properly, her left arm stitches were starting to close well, and she could pivot a little better with the leg brace. She learned what worked best for her to help the moving go easier. Her colorful room full of art, cards, flowers and stuffed bears were all packed up and ready to go. We were both excited to go home. Transportation was set up and Daysha left rehab to come home for the first time since the accident! It was a proud moment to witness as a parent.

When the transportation company brought Daysha into our house, there was one step that they had to get the wheelchair up on, then push her into the house. I did not think of needing a ramp for the wheelchair. No one told us of all the things we needed to have for the recovery phase. There was plenty of trial and error many times. The first thing we did was go right back outside to take Daysha around the neighborhood. We pushed her wheelchair down the sidewalk on this breezy sunny day in September 2019. She truly enjoyed being outdoors. I didn't realize that not all sidewalks are made equally. Some were mid-lined while others crooked and had a big hump. About twenty minutes into the walk Daysha said her back hurt. Every bump was uncomfortable due to uneven sidewalks. So we tried pushing the wheelchair in the street close to the sidewalk. She could not stay straight up for long in the wheelchair because it was a generic one that did not have reclining options. We got her back home and into the hospital bed as soon as possible.

That evening I realized that I could not sleep upstairs in my bed because Daysha would need help getting onto the bedside toilet, turning onto her side, something to drink or anything else she needed throughout the night. So we both moved into the living room and I slept on the couch.

There was no how to trauma survivor guide out, until now! So every day we experienced something different and figured it out for ourselves. I learned every day how to do things better. I remember Daysha wanted to paint every day. We put her on the couch with lots of pillows to prop her back up, and set up the paint on a dinner fold out table. You can be creative and use what you have to make things work for yourself. She made some of her most memorable artwork on that couch!

Your insurance should cover the at home therapy with limits to two or three times a week. This will be set up before you leave the hospital or rehabilitation center along with follow up visits to your doctor. The at home version of the Physical and Occupational Therapist each came three times a week to make sure Daysha was healing properly. They used things from around the house like my kitchen towels rolled up to prop her knee, a water bottle as a weight, silly putty for strengthening, stretch bands, and an exercise ball to help lift her foot etc. With all these things and the daily exercises, Daysha did to learn how to use her arms and legs again properly, I could see how determined she was to get back to normal.

Debbie the therapist was awesome. She had a heart for her work skills. I truly appreciate the patience she had with Daysha and the work she needed in certain areas too. Not being in the gym did not matter to Debbie. She had Daysha workout in the chair just as if she was at the gym a few hours three days a week. We began to look forward to therapy which became the highlight of our day. The necessity to do those exercises was high so she could walk again.

I learned that after surgery the healing process without movement only promotes scar tissue and pain. Scar tissue is a collection of cells that grow to cover the site of the injury or surgery as it heals. It can grow both inside or outside the wound. When scar tissue grows, it is the natural way our bodies respond to heal the wound. It has less elasticity than skin, so it causes tightness, limited movement and pain. The way to reduce scar tissue pain or swelling is to massage the area, moisturize the scar, and exercise that body part as often as possible. Consistency is the key! There would be a day or two that Daysha did not feel like doing her stretches or exercises and that's when you have to encourage your loved one to just do it! I will say it is not always smooth sailing; some challenging times came too.

I would get tired from all the physical labor it took to just help my daughter do one thing. At night I would be totally knocked out sleeping! Daysha would have to yell "MOM! I need help" to wake me up because she needed to turn from one side to the other to get comfortable. Or she would have to use the bathroom. I remember one time jumping up out of my sleep with an attitude because I had to get her onto the toilet. She had been calling me for a while. I was frustrated and she was too. She did not want to wake me up but could not get onto the bedside toilet herself. Could you imagine how that feels as the injured person does not want to ask for help but has to ask anyway? We both just yelled at each other out of frustration. I apologized immediately afterwards because this is what I was here for as a parent. It was not the time to get into my own feelings and it was not about me. As her parent, I would take care of her no matter how tired I was. I quickly got my emotions together to help her move. I told you this is real but it is an example of some of the rough times you may experience. It was okay to express how we felt to each other minus the yelling. It will not always be a happy time but you can get through it with the right attitude and heart posture. Roman 5:3-5 encourages us in this, for it says our trials build perseverance and perseverance build character. It changed the way I looked at life. From then on, I would get up the second she called for help.

It was time for Daysha's first doctor's appointment since the accident. We did not know what to expect. She was okay riding in the front seat of the car. I drove slowly as Mrs Daisy on the road, more nervous about her first ride in the car than she was. We had to go to Radiology to get pictures of all her bones before we saw the doctor. This is the career field I am very familiar with in my years working in this profession. It would take a while because we basically radiated her whole body except her head. I knew all the positions and even helped her hold for them as they took the pictures. With modern technology, the digital pictures came up immediately onto the computer screen.

You know the feeling of your stomach as you first go down the top of the hill on a roller coaster? That's the feeling I got as I saw all my daughter's bones with metal rods, pins, plates and screws going through each bone in her body. I was totally shocked. I had seen this over and over so many times in all kinds of other people for years. It became routine to see broken bones and hardware from surgery. But it is totally different when it hits home. My baby girl, the one I carried in my belly for nine months, watched grow up into this beautiful young lady, who was now filled with metal pieces and parts. Those metal pieces and parts were holding her bones back together again as they were healing. I held my breath and couldn't breathe for a few seconds. I could not start crying right there even though I wanted to. Daysha, however, was doing well as she lay on the x-ray table and held the positions needed. I took in a deep breath, blew all the air out and kept encouraging her on how well she was doing. My facial expression was stuck on smiling but I was crying on the inside. I cried because the radiographs actually put into more perspective for me how I had almost lost my daughter.

I did not have time to let myself go down that depressing rabbit hole. There will be times your emotions will try to come back up and it's okay but do not let them take over. There's a time to cry, there's a time to laugh, as Ecclesiastes 3:4 advises. Just be mindful of when it's the right time for those emotions. I am not saying you cannot cry or be emotional. I am simply saying don't let yourself get out of control and go into depression. So I kept smiling as we waited in the next exam room.

In came this nice handsome doctor and his team of student doctors. He introduced himself as Dr. Halman. I found out he was one of the top Orthopedic Trauma surgeons at MG Level 1 Trauma Hospital. He said that he was happy to see Daysha and asked how the healing exercises were going. He explained everything about the healing process based on the recent radiographs she'd just taken. He stressed that it was very important for her to push those exercises if she wanted to start learning how to walk correctly again. He explained how scar tissue can form and stiffen up all the parts of the body where she had surgery. It can become hardened, painful and unable to bend at the joints. All she had to do to avoid scar tissue build up was move everyday! You must do those exercises several times a day after the therapist leaves your house. Make it fun by adding music or have someone do them with you but just do it!

We were so thankful that Mick's parents waited to do his funeral just so both ladies could heal and attend. Unfortunately, Cathy was not healed enough to attend, so her mother came to represent her. Mick was cremated and his funeral service was so touching, more like a life celebration of Mick. There were tears but more laughter listening to all the stories people told about him. Mick touched so many people's lives through his heart to share love. I watched to see if this was too much of a mental strain for Daysha. However, she proved to be fine. I believe it was crucial for her to be there. As I pushed her around in the wheelchair, it was good to see her talking to all their friends and even seeing a few of the rescuers from that night. Daysha was able to be placed in the front row by his parents' side.

She had shared with them a past conversation she had with Mick about how they would plan their funerals. Mick had said he knew people would be sad but he wanted everyone to celebrate his life. And they must play Drake songs throughout the whole funeral. With no idea of the tragic accident coming a few months after that conversation, Daysha was able to tell Mick's parents about his wishes for the funeral. Daysha spoke more of the many great times they spent together and how she would miss him deeply. That is a precious memory I will always have in my heart.

How it Happened

This is the part that took me so long to write. Pre-warning, the details are mildly graphic. These were things we learned from witnesses about the accident. When Mick was driving home he was behind a truck and another car was on the side of him. The drunk driver got onto the freeway exit the wrong way traveling at 100 mph. As he narrowly missed several cars, many people started calling into 911 to report him. At this time with Mick driving, Candy on the front passenger side, Cathy on the back driver side and Daysha on the back passenger side asleep, they had no clue what was coming straight up ahead. As the drunk driver continued, the truck in front of their car swerved out of the way and Mick only had seconds to make the decision to try to swerve out of the way too. Candy only had seconds to yell,"Mick watch out!" as the drunk driver's car smashed into her side first. The head on collision killed Candy and the drunk driver instantly.

Mick was unconscious. Cathy was awake as her head lay on Daysha's lap with an internally decapitated skull from her neck. She couldn't move but could see the back of Mick's head. Daysha was awakened from her sleep as her legs were smashed backwards into broken pieces like the shape of the letter W. Daysha screamed at the top of her lungs until she passed out from the shock. Both young ladies had several broken bones in their body as they lay there helpless until help would soon come.

A few witnesses tried to pry open the car door to get all the teenagers out of the car., I believe God did not allow those doors to open because, although the witnesses meant well, one wrong move could have caused them to be in a worse condition such as being paralyzed. I believe that God allowed Cathy's head to be placed in the correct position on top of Daysha's broken legs just so she could stay alive. When Daysha stated that Mick told her everything would be okay, we know that could not have possibly happened because he was unconscious on impact and she passed out. I believe with all my heart, body and soul that God allowed Daysha to see Mick's spirit come to her to tell her that she would be okay.

An off duty Ambulance company stopped to help get all the teenagers stabilized as best they could until the first responders got to the scene to move them. I believe God had them passing by at that exact moment. Due to legalities, I cannot mention who they are but I truly am thankful that you stopped to help. Because of all the first responders, both girls were able to hang onto hope for survival. Both of these young ladies are truly strong walking miracles today. I am so inspired by them!

CHAPTER 9

Strive To Be Alive

THE BIBLICAL MEANING OF the number nine is the divine completeness of God and a symbol of finality. Nine is the number of surgeries Daysha had done. God completely restored her body back to the living! Her body was healing at an accelerated rate to the amazement of the doctors. Though we were far from the ending of this trauma, things got better to tolerate as we learned ways to navigate through this new way of life. Therapy, doctor visits and Daysha's artwork became part of our normal routine.

Through my entire Christian journey, I have learned the power of thanking God even when things are not doing so well in your life. As time passed, it was apparent that my daughter was being restored and we gained more confidence in the entire process. For me, in particular, after experiencing the struggle of helping a person healing from the accident, my perspective and empathy grew stronger for trauma conquerors. Yes, you and your loved one are more than trauma conquerors! You must make sure to get your arm muscles strong, ready to help your loved one. You, as the helper, have to carry plenty of bags to have things they need. Wheelchair your loved one to the car, help get them in, break down the wheelchair, put it in the trunk, then get in the car to drive around looking for the closest parking spot near the door.

I did not mind doing this routine. However I did mind the parking lot wars, especially trying to find a nearby parking space when going to her doctor appointments. I would see someone perfectly healthy rush to put their car into a parking spot right next to the door as I sadly drove by thinking to myself don't they see this handicapped sticker on the car?! Don't they know how much work it takes to get my loved one in and out of the car? No! No! And No! That person has no clue what you are experiencing and definitely did not see the sticker on the front of the car. In today's world so many people limit their focus to just themselves and what is going on only in their life. I am guilty of this too. We as human beings have to try to do better. I actually gained more respect for those handicapped parking spaces and people who have the stickers! I too was guilty of parking in a handicapped space for a quick minute just because I was in a rush. I officially apologize to all those people that really do need those parking spots. It's hard to walk far or push the wheelchair from a distant parking space to get into a building. Please become more thoughtful of those people in need.

In today's world it is appreciated that there are people who really care for others and want to help. Many people want to help those in need but just do not know how to contribute. Being in a helpless position, we were thankful for any kind of help we got. It did not matter if it was time spent on visiting us, prayers, food, clothes, toiletries, gifts cards, money or just sending love because we were grateful. Usually you hear about a tragedy on the news and about a week later it's all forgotten. It blew my mind that people thought of us two months after the accident.

Many people's hearts were so touched by the trauma of these four innocent kids that the whole city of Twinsburg and other people from other cities came out to support us at an event. The event was called The Twinsburg Hearts 4 Healing. The mayor of Twinsburg, some of the first responders, our families, friends, lawyers and a few news channels were all there to support us. Our lawyer was always available to give advice and direct us on the legalities of our situation. It was a blessing to see so many people of every ethnicity come together in love to help the best way they knew how. You may not really feel like having people around if you are vulnerable, broken-hearted or still experiencing pain. However, it is the best therapy for your heart to experience at some point. Let people help you if they want to. Do not let pride or shame get in your way!

Our community came together as one city to raise money for all four families. There was a concert of local bands that donated their time to perform on an outdoor stage. Local food and other businesses donated basket raffles, baked goods and give-aways. The bar that hosted the event had a special area for the families to be together. All the proceeds would be split up among performers, event rentals and all four families. A month later each family got $5,000 to help out with any needs. That may not seem like a lot of money to some, but it was such a huge blessing to us. It helped our family survive.

I quickly learned that when you are on FMLA from your job for your nineteen year old child, it does not cover you for short term disability. I was told, because the accident did not happen to me, I could not get paid. I did not know how I would get food, pay rent, utilities bills, cell phone etc. I dreaded the thought of having to go back to work and leave my daughter for someone else to take care of her. How? Who? What? When? These thoughts were on my mind, plus the added stress of getting the FMLA paperwork correct.

You know how you just want to stay in your bed for the day? Or how you just want to turn off the world for a few days to figure out some things all by yourself? I felt this way but it was totally wrong thinking! Do not fall for the voices in your head that tell you things like, "I need to be all alone. I am a private person. I cannot ask people for help. Nobody cares about my problems or it's always going to be like this always."

Those negative voices you hear do not come from God. The bible warns us *"Be sober-minded; be watchful. Your adversary the devil prowls around like a roaring lion, seeking someone to devour"* (1 Peter 5:8). But God always works things out for the good in every situation. You might not understand, or see the ending or know how to manage all that stress. But just keep hope, keep faith and know you will make it through.

And I was in for another pleasant surprise. Without my knowledge, Apostle Greg called for an emergency meeting after church service. He asked people to help me with caring for Daysha when I had to go back to work. How did he know? It could only have been God that put the thought in his heart. I was so appreciative and thankful that Mother Sandra and Pastor Denise both volunteered to help be sitters at no cost. Yes, you read that right… out of their hearts and free of charge! God does indeed meet all of my needs as He promises in Philippians 4:19.

I already had help from my parents, brothers, sister, daughter from another mother Theandra and Daysha's friend Jarrett and his mom LaTerra because they all helped daily at the hospital since the first day. But I did not want to burn them all out. They also had work and other things going on in their own lives even if they wanted to help every day. It was such a relief for me to have more surprise help from Daysha's dad, my neighbors The Thomas's, the Clevelands and a few other close friends. I scheduled days and times for each person to come help out as I went back to work.

My Transition to Work

Going back to work was very uncomfortable at first. All I wanted to do was get to work, keep my head down and get done so I could leave and be home with my baby girl. Of course it was the opposite! I ran into every coworker I could think of that wanted to talk. People I didn't even know came to find me to say sorry, or ask how my daughter was doing. I smiled and repeated myself continuously throughout the day while suppressing the urge to suddenly cry out loud. It was like that night of getting the phone call all over again each time I had to talk about it over and over.

I started to lose my patience, get very short with people or suddenly change the subject. Of course, my coworkers were only trying to show compassion, care and support. Although a few people may seem to just be nosy, most of the time it comes from the good intentions of their heart. I had no reason to get frustrated. So do not allow yourself to get into that place.

I was the helper in this traumatic situation but did not realize how much I was affected by the trauma too. I would assure everyone I was fine but on the inside I was not fine. As a result, my emotions were high so I would get upset easily. I would run to the bathroom crying my eyes out, then go back to work right afterwards like nothing had happened. Make sure to be very aware of your emotions. When you first get back out into the public eye, you may want to express that you do not want to talk about the traumatic accident. It is okay for you to say that you do not want to discuss things, while giving a short update to people you are okay. Be honest with yourself and others.

    I thank God that He was with me every step of the way because through it all, He kept me mentally stable. It took time for me to get used to being back to my work routine. I could no longer hold in my feelings that I was so disappointed that I was forced to be back at work due to the financial need. I felt terrible leaving my daughter at home with someone else and I was emotionally exhausted. My mind could only focus on my daughter at home in the hospital bed. I believe this challenge is another part of the healing process too. As the helper of the loved one who experienced the trauma, you must be patient with yourself. Be able to acknowledge that you cannot do everything alone. You too can become burnt out physically and emotionally. Speak over yourself 2 Timothy 1:7: *"God has not given me a spirit of fear but of power, love and a sound mind"* because words are spirit and they are life.

    It is so important to prepare yourself before going back out into a public setting. Some things you can do are to talk about your feelings even if you're just talking to God alone. You can meditate, write your feelings in a journal, pray, join a support group or start a new activity. This will allow you to channel all those emotions to a healthy place as you navigate through the process. Remember, if you're the trauma conqueror or the helper of your loved one, the negative or discouraging things are there to distract you. The distraction comes to keep you broken-hearted, depressed or try to make you give up. You are in control of your choice to have healing.

Some people say they use the law of attraction by receiving in return what they give out into the universe. I know from my own experiences in this traumatic situation, that it was just God. He IS the law that attracts good things! All things ARE working together for your good in every part (the good and the bad) of your situation. How is the bad part working for your good? Because you learn something from it and it changes your perspective of things in your situation. You then appreciate how far you've come because you can see evidence of your healing. Your story is real and the things you have encountered make you stronger, more understanding and knowledgeable in your situation. You are now better able to help someone who is experiencing what you have already been through.

Daysha poses as live art at UM College 2021

CHAPTER 10

Begin at the End

"CELEBRATE GOOD TIMES COME on duh nuh nuh nuh nuh nuh nuh, yahoo…let's celebrate!" If I could play a song for you right now, that would be playing! I celebrate you for coming along with me through this traumatic experience. I thank you, the reader and supporter because getting this information out to people is important to me. Traumatic experiences change the lives of both the trauma conqueror and their loved ones who are there to support them. Trauma leaves a person feeling naked inside and out, unable to clothe yourself until you sew your own blanket of safety around you to feel safe again. But patience leads to a time of restoration that brings joy back into your life!

Other surprises God gave us were definitely signs, wonders and miracles in today's world. A few of my coworkers got together to donate paid time off hours just so I could get a paycheck. It was enough to pay my rent and a few bills. One of the well known doctors pressed an envelope full of money into my hand and said, "Don't say a word; just accept it, please." Another family member gave us an envelope full of money to pay rent and a car note. All the gift cards helped us to have food to eat. We received several unexpected deliveries of wellness baskets, edible fruit, blankets and cards. I was more than overwhelmed because of the great support and love we received from coworkers from both my old and current job, family, friends and strangers. This was all God's way of showing us what happens when we believe, depend on and trust in Him. Believe me, we needed and used everything that was given but God already knew exactly what we would need. We want to thank everyone for their contributions. We're so blessed and appreciative!

First New Steps

Two months had gone by when I finally got to see Debbie the physical therapist help Daysha take her first steps to walk again! It was like watching her at eleven months old again. I cried as I videoed her slowly step one foot at a time while holding onto a cane. She walked from our kitchen to her hospital bed in our living room about six feet away. A few weeks before Daysha took her first steps, so did Cathy at the nursing home with a walker as her therapist guided her through. Her mom recorded her too! What moments of joy and tears to see these two young ladies learn to do simple things like lift their leg or arm!

These two young ladies were healing together while in different facilities. They were determined to be healed and whole again 100 percent. It took a lot of hard work but they did it. The positive speaking proved to work well for Daysha.

On Daysha's twentieth birthday, she walked with a cane into the Cleveland City Hall to see all the first responders that saved both their lives! Both ladies were able to walk into the ceremony, meet, thank and hug each one of the first responders as they received awards of recognition. It was such a surreal moment for everyone. The mayor of Cleveland then took both families to tour and see historical places inside of his city hall office. What a birthday gift!

Now two years later, plus a pandemic, Daysha is now able to ride her bike, do stretches, work, always paint or do other artwork, be in the marching band, and attend college in the state of Florida! She has a totally new perspective on life. She shows it through her lifestyle by choosing to live with as many of her heart's desires as she can accomplish. In October 2020, Daysha opened her own online art business called Watajii. Her first art gallery show was at the Cleveland House of Blues where she showed stunning art pieces and art clothing commissions that were sold. She decided not to tell about her near death experience as she wanted to be known for her artwork, not for her trauma. I believe the experience has heightened her creativity at a higher level as she has so much more to do and see in life.

Daysha is a strong inspiration to me and I am so proud of the young lady she has become. I will always remember when Daysha said, "This trauma is only a moment." I have learned so much through it too. I will have more empathy for those who don't show their pain. I will not judge others so quickly because I do not know about them; but they too have a story to tell. I just have to take time to stop and listen.

Daysha and Cathy grew closer as friends. We are thankful that they have each other to talk to about all they went through. Only they can truly understand it all from their own experience as the trauma conquerors: "Yet in all these things we are more than conquerors through Him who loved us" (Romans 8:37).

Cathy is going to college, working, driving and living her life. I am so proud of the young lady she has become through this trauma. She has shown tremendous strength and continues to live her life filled with the love of her family. Mick's family is always remembering Mick and taking one day at a time, continuing to live instead of choosing to stay in grief. They have generous hearts that just want to share love to all Mick's friends by allowing all of them to come over and stay in touch. They are working on a short film that talks about Mick's life and both young ladies are in it as trauma conquerors. Candy's family is taking it day by day too to keep her lovely smile and personality in remembrance of all the lives she touched. Her mother has a wonderful garden that has a stone of remembrance for Candy.

I hope that you were blessed by reading this book and it touched your heart in some way. I pray for you to have a deeper understanding of people who experience trauma and the process that it takes to make it through.

I will leave you with this last prayer: "I decree and declare that you and your loved ones will be healed just as quickly as my daughter was. You are free as He heals your broken heart and binds up your wounds (Psalm 103:3). I decree that you and your loved ones will be made totally whole with no residue of anything broken spirituality, mentally and physically, in Jesus' mighty name. Amen!"

About the Author

DELICIA MAYES IS A Radiologic and Magnetic Resonance Technologist, Author, Motivational Speaker, Ministry Leader and Single Mother. Delicia started writing short stories in elementary school. By fifth grade she won a writing contest that awarded her with over 200 books! She loves writing, reading, art, music, family and laughter.. Her only daughter has become an artist and is currently in college at University of Miami in Florida.

Delicia joined New Beginning Ministries in 2017 because of the strong faith, family and fellowship! She loves the vision of a Real God for real people with real issues! Delicia has grown into ministry leadership, administration, the finance team and choir. She has contributed author pieces in four books with Apostle and Senior Pastor McCurry, two other collaborations with other authors, and is currently publishing her own next book!

Delicia has worked in the hospital's Radiology Department for eighteen years. She has a passion for encouraging people through their toughest moments in life by seeing God's work in everything! We have all experienced something not so pleasant or may not have been easy BUT you made it through! You have a purpose, position and attestation in life and now is your moment of restoration! Delicia will help you get there with God's guidance. Book Delicia for speaking events, teaching, workshops and trauma restoration.

> **Isaiah 41:10 NIV:**
>
> So do not fear, for I am with you; do not be dismayed, for I am your God. I will strengthen you and help you; I will uphold you with my righteous right hand.

Contact information:
Email: AuthorDeliciaMMayes@gmail.com

Social Media
Facebook ~ Delicia Mayes
Instagram ~ @Deeleecee_a
LinkedIn ~ Delicia Mayes

Endnotes

1. Thomas Nelson, Inc. Holy Bible, New King James Version (NKJV). 1982

2. Charles Dickens quote about hope https://www.goodreads.com/toggle_mobile © 2022 Goodreads, Inc Desktop version

3. HIPPA Law – https://en.m.wikipedia.org/wiki/Health_Insurance_Portability_and_Accountability_Act#cite_ref-3

Watajii Online Art Store
by Daysha Watson.

Website: Watajii.etsy.com
Contact : Instagram: @watajii_
Email: watajiix@gmail.com

Now is always the time for oneself

I am Day W. I tend to create art that raises questions and are open to numerous interpretations.
I am currently selling prints, posters and clothing commissions.
I had a near death experience where everything, including my creativity were jeopardized and almost taken away. So now, happy and shining, I have decided to live by my creativity, not by the world. If I have learned one thing, it's that there is no better moment than this one right now to start doing what makes you happy.

McCurry Ministries International Publishing Assistance

Serving God's People, Telling Their Story

We're an impact-driven author assistant publishing firm, specializing in author branding and development. Our books showcase literature which Promote Biblical principles for change and personal transformation.

TERESA MCCURRY
CEO

GREGORY MCCURRY
President

2060 West 65th Street Cleveland, Ohio 44102
MMI.serving.people@gmail.com | www.NBFellowshipInt.org
(216) 916-9270 ext. 4

www.ingramcontent.com/pod-product-compliance
Lightning Source LLC
Chambersburg PA
CBHW042309150426
43198CB00001B/14